SEEING THINGS SIMPLY

COLOR

LESSONS & EXERCISES TO DEVELOP
YOUR PAINTING & DRAWING TECHNIQUE

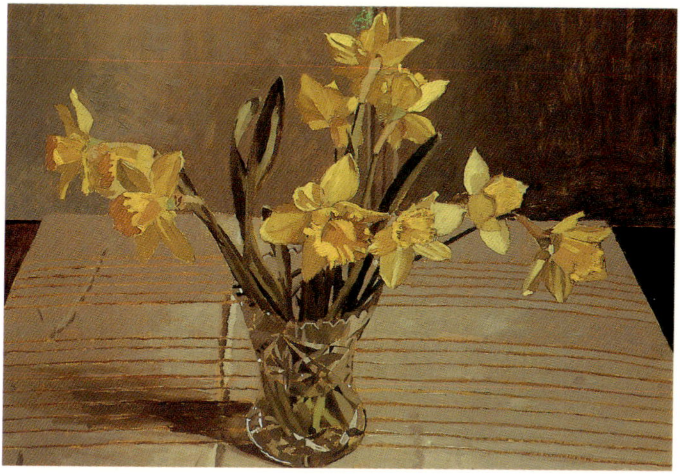

JEREMY GALTON

CHARTWELL
BOOKS, INC.

A QUINTET BOOK

Published by Chartwell Books
A Division of Book Sales, Inc.
110 Enterprise Avenue
Secaucus, New Jersey 07094

This edition produced for sale
in the U.S.A., its territories
and dependencies only.

ISBN 0-7858-0125-1

This book was designed and produced by
Quintet Publishing Limited
6 Blundell Street
London N7 9BH

Creative Director: Richard Dewing
Designer: Ian Hunt
Project Editor: Helen Denholm
Editor: Hazel Harrison
Photographer: Paul Forrester

Typeset in Great Britain by
Central Southern Typesetters, Eastbourne
Manufactured in Singapore by
Eray Scan Pte Ltd
Printed in China

Contents

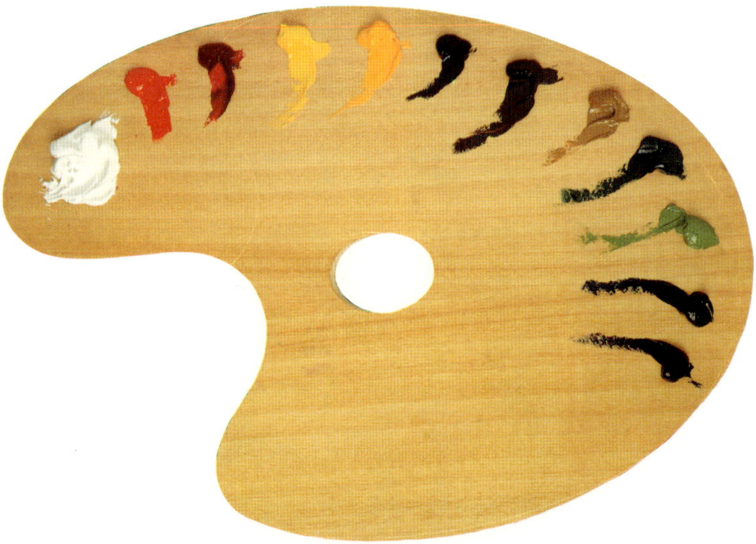

INTRODUCTION

LEARNING TO MIX colors is one of the most difficult aspects of painting, at least initially, although it becomes easier the more you practice. In this book I have suggested various ways of giving yourself this hands-on experience – there are color charts you can use as a basis for your own experiments, and there are some exercises you might like to try out. I have also shown several of my own paintings and explained which colors I have used.

Color is, of course, not only about mixing. You need to understand the relationships of colors, too. Colors do not exist in a vacuum; they are affected by the quality of the light as well as by surrounding colors. Whole books have been written about color theory, but here I have restricted theory to a minimum, providing what I hope are helpful hints on how colors behave.

The paintings and charts shown in this book are in oils, as this is the medium in which I work, but color is color whatever medium you use, and those who work in acrylics, pastels, or watercolors will still find the advice useful. Watercolorists must remember, however, that because oil is an opaque medium, colors are lightened by adding white. In watercolor, which is transparent, colors are lightened by using them more thinly – the white being that of the paper.

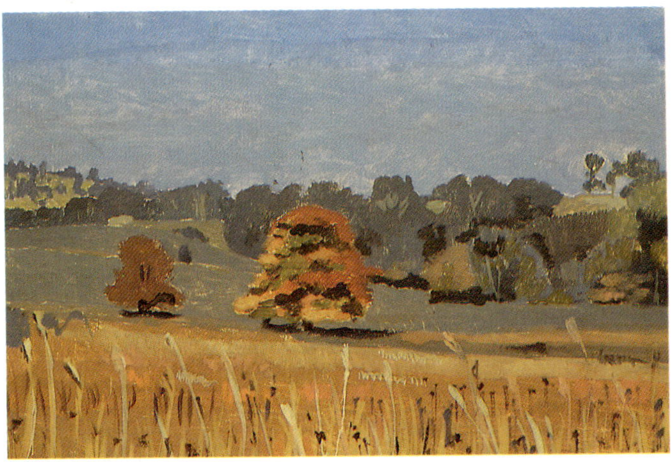

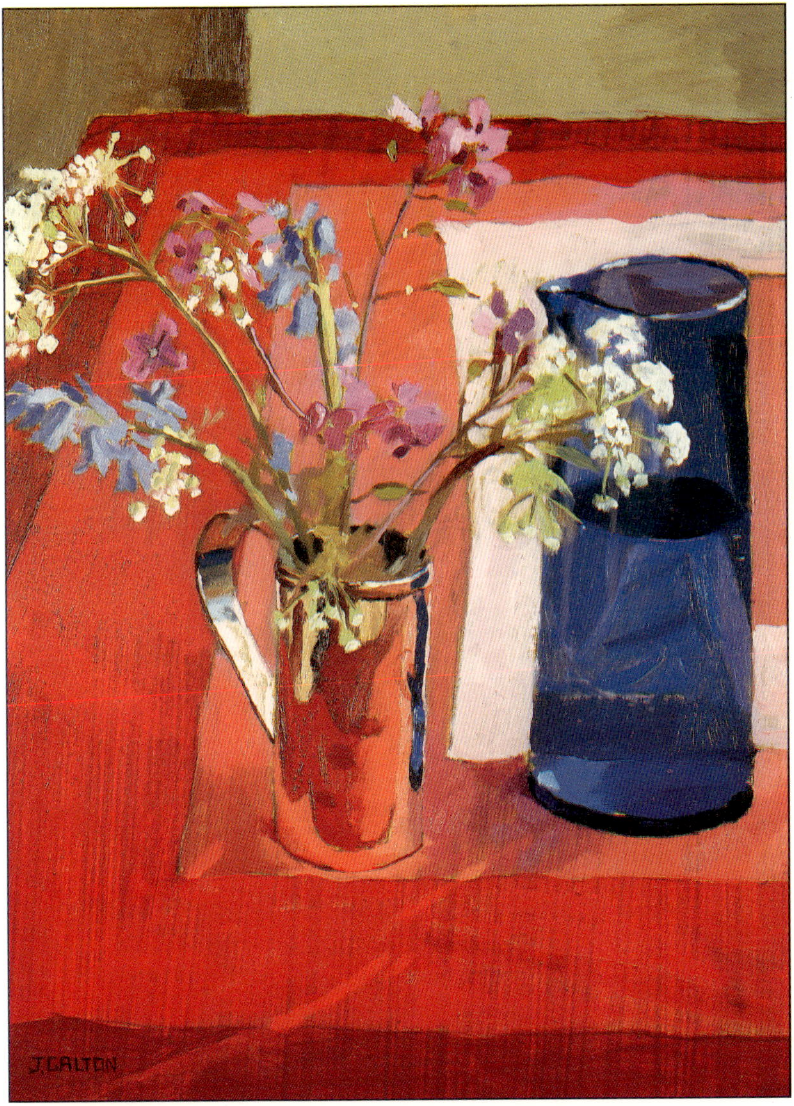
J.GALTON

THE PRIMARY COLORS

WHATEVER OTHER COLORS you decide to include in your paintbox, there are three essential ones that you must have. These are the primary colors – red, yellow, and blue – so called because they cannot be produced from mixtures of other colors. Pairs of these colors are mixed together to produce the secondary colors: red and yellow make orange, blue and yellow make green, and red and blue make purple.

RIGHT
Cadmium red and cadmium yellow make a strong, clear orange; the blue and yellow mixture is useful for subtle greens, and the blue and red for purplish browns. For true purple, ultramarine needs to be mixed with alizarin crimson.

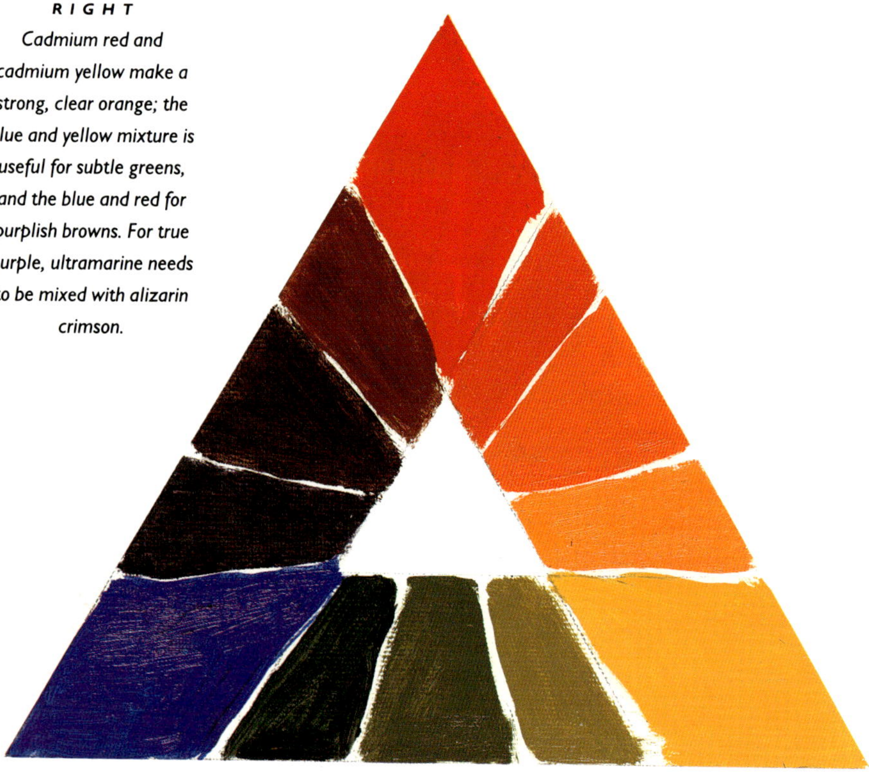

To make a full range of secondaries you need at least two of each primary, because there are different versions of each one. To mix vivid oranges, greens, and purples you need to choose the two primaries that have a "bias" towards one another. If you make color "triangles" like the ones shown here, you will quickly discover how this works. You can see, for example, that cadmium red and cadmium yellow make a good orange, but that cadmium red and ultramarine do not make a true purple, but a brownish one instead. Purple is a difficult color to mix. An ultramarine and alizarin crimson mixture makes a very dark purple, so you may need to add a touch of white.

Alizarin crimson

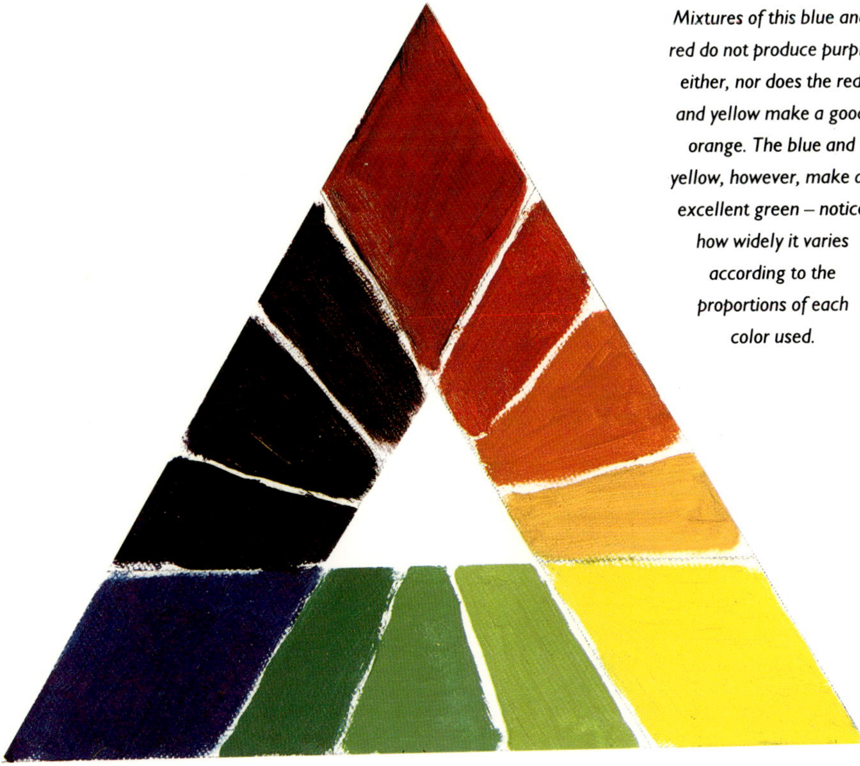

Winsor (phthalocyanine) blue

Lemon yellow

LEFT
Mixtures of this blue and red do not produce purple either, nor does the red and yellow make a good orange. The blue and yellow, however, make an excellent green – notice how widely it varies according to the proportions of each color used.

EXTENDING THE RANGE

THE RANGE OF secondary colors you can make from mixtures of the primaries becomes far greater when you add black and white. These charts are an extended version of the triangles shown on the previous pages, with increasing proportions of black and white added to the secondary colors; you can see the

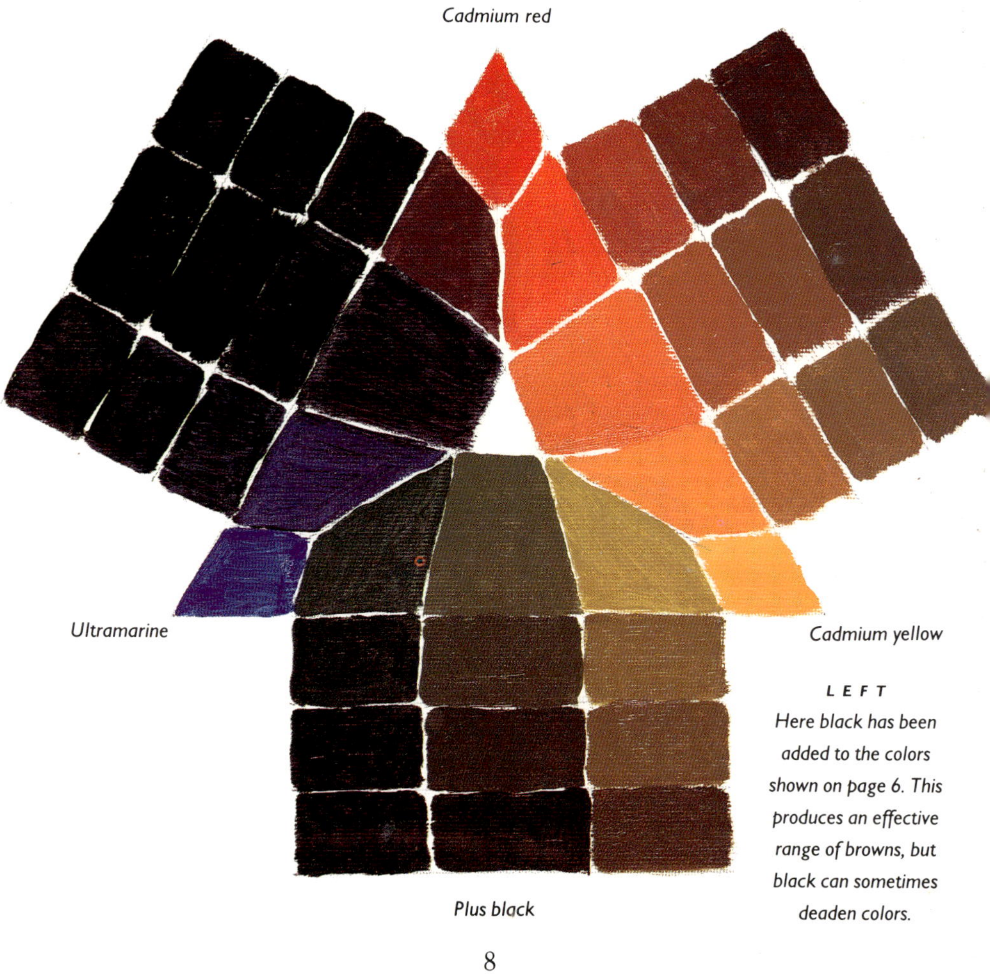

LEFT
Here black has been added to the colors shown on page 6. This produces an effective range of browns, but black can sometimes deaden colors.

primaries in the corners. You can learn a great deal by doing mixing exercises like these – and it is fun. Notice, in particular, the beautifully subtle colors achieved by adding white to the "wrong" primary mixtures, such as alizarin crimson and lemon yellow. This mixture could be perfect for skin tones.

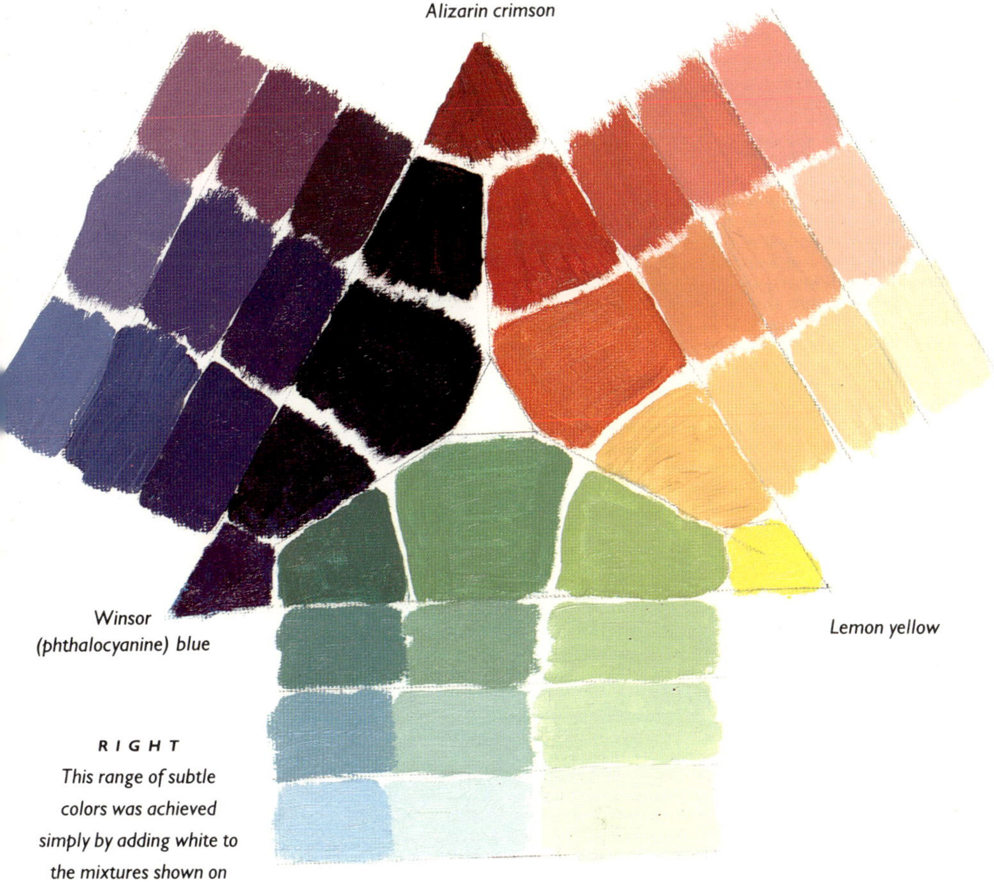

RIGHT
This range of subtle colors was achieved simply by adding white to the mixtures shown on page 7.

THE EFFECT OF WHITE

WHEN YOU ARE using opaque paint you nearly always have to use a little white, but in some cases this can change the nature of the colors. As you can see from these color "swatches," it is perfectly safe to add white to yellow and blue, but red becomes pink as soon as it is diluted with even a small amount of

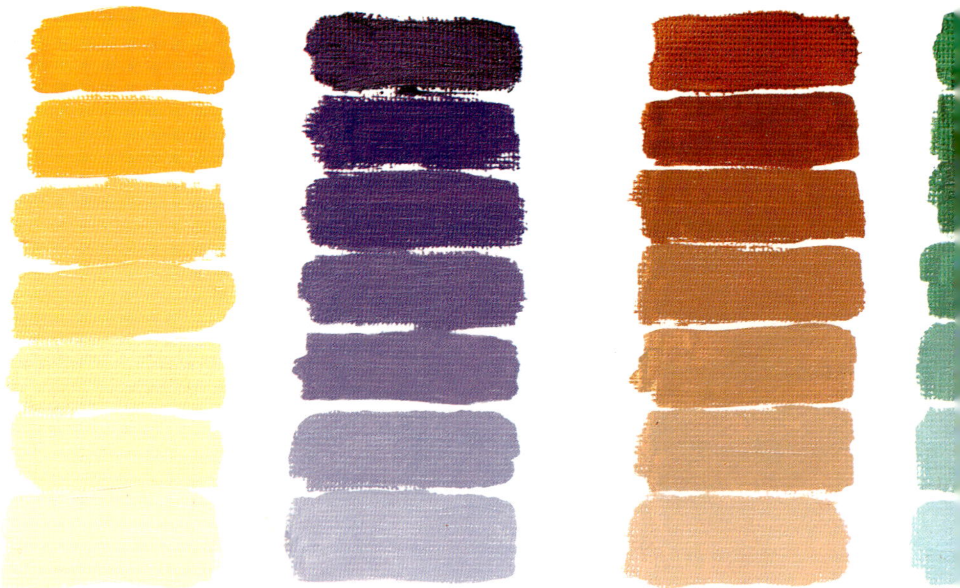

Cadmium yellow

Winsor violet

Burnt sienna

Viridi

white. Here it can be more satisfactory to use small quantities of yellow – but not too much or you will, of course, have orange. Viridian also undergoes a change, becoming progressively bluer as more white is mixed with it. When you practice color mixing, try to remember such effects, as they may come in handy when you are painting. Viridian mixed with some white, for example, could prove to be the ideal color for sea, which is often a combination of blue-greens and deep blues and purples.

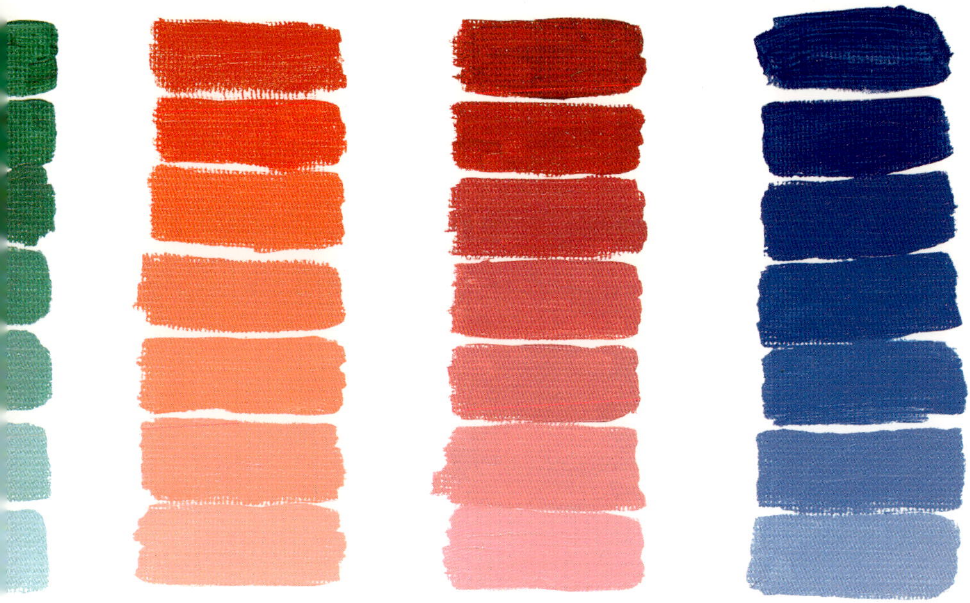

Cadmium red *Alizarin crimson* *Ultramarine*

ABOVE

When you are working with opaque paints such as oils or acrylics, you will nearly always need to use some white, but be aware that it can change the character of certain colors, turning red into pink for example.

THE EFFECT OF BLACK

ADDING BLACK also changes colors, and in a more dramatic fashion than adding white does. Black and yellow become green, while black added to red makes brown. If you want to retain the character of the color it is often better to find other ways of darkening colors. You could try darkening red with

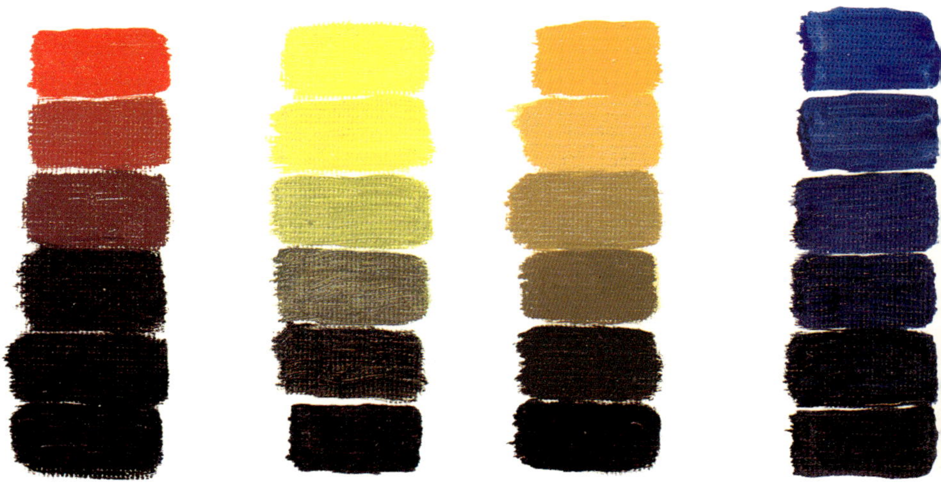

ABOVE

Black can also change the character of a color. Black and red makes brown, and black and yellow an interesting range of greens. These effects are shown in the three swatches on the left. The others suggest some alternative ways of darkening colors.

touches of blue or brown, for example. Yellow is a naturally light color, but if you are painting a yellow object there will be some dark shadow areas; unless you want green shadows, the best idea is to darken the color with brown, perhaps with a little red added.

Some artists ban black from their palettes altogether, but I find it a very useful color. Greens made by mixing black and yellow are quite unlike any blue-yellow mixtures, and adding black to blue and purples produces very rich, deep colors.

Cadmium red

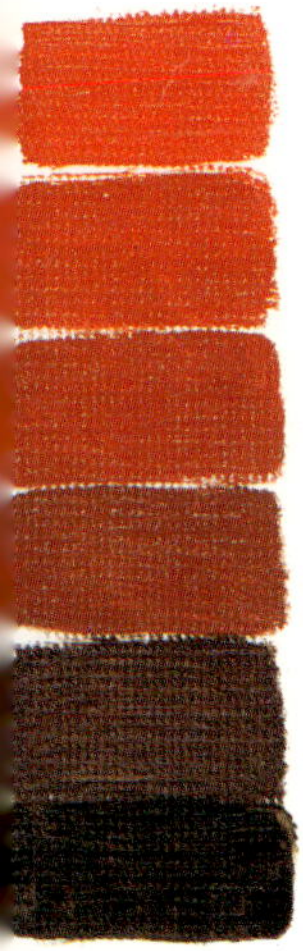

Raw umber

Cadmium red

Alizarin crimson

Lemon yellow

Raw umber

Cadmium yellow

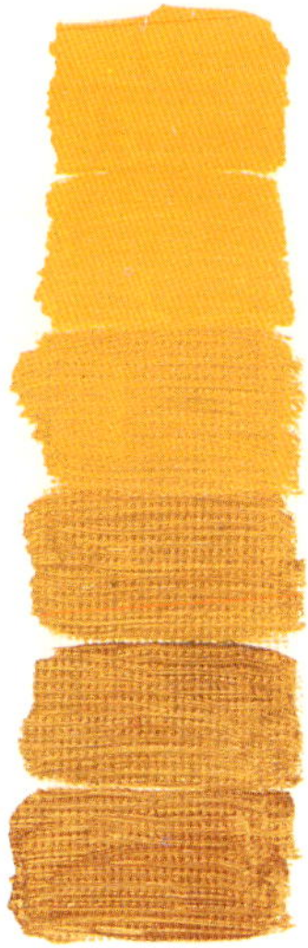

Raw sienna

USING THREE COLORS

AN EXERCISE often set in art schools is that of painting with a limited palette of three primary colors. This forces you to concentrate on color mixing, and illustrates what can and cannot be done with these basic colors. Both these small studies have been done with three colors plus white. As you will see, in one I have been unable to achieve satisfactory mixtures for either the

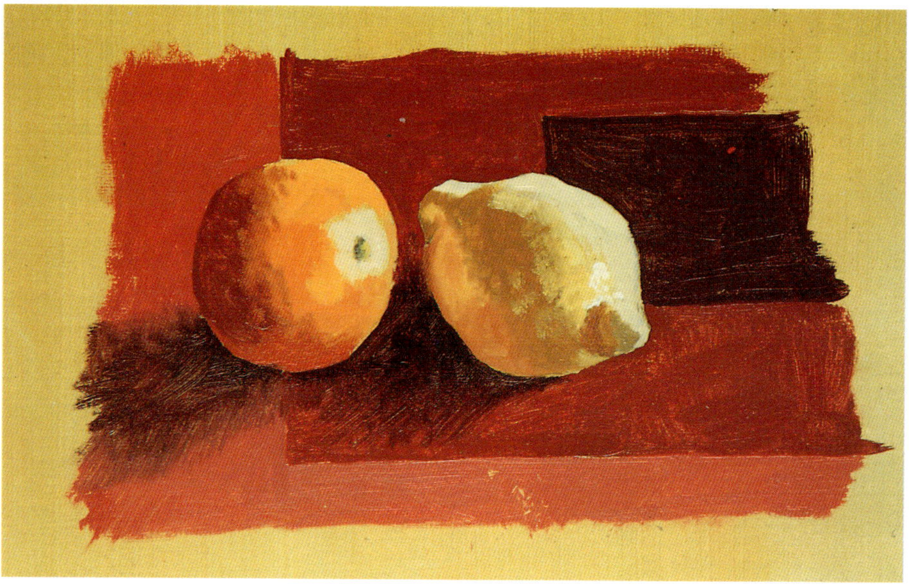

ABOVE

I have used ultramarine, cadmium red, cadmium yellow, and white. While the red and yellow make a strong, true orange, the color of the cloth is muddy, and the lemon lacks vitality.

lemon or the crimson cloth, while in the second the orange is the weak point because lemon yellow and alizarin crimson simply do not make orange. In a way, this is a negative exercise, because you are finding out what you cannot do. On pages 16–17 all six primaries have been used, giving considerably more scope for accurate color mixing.

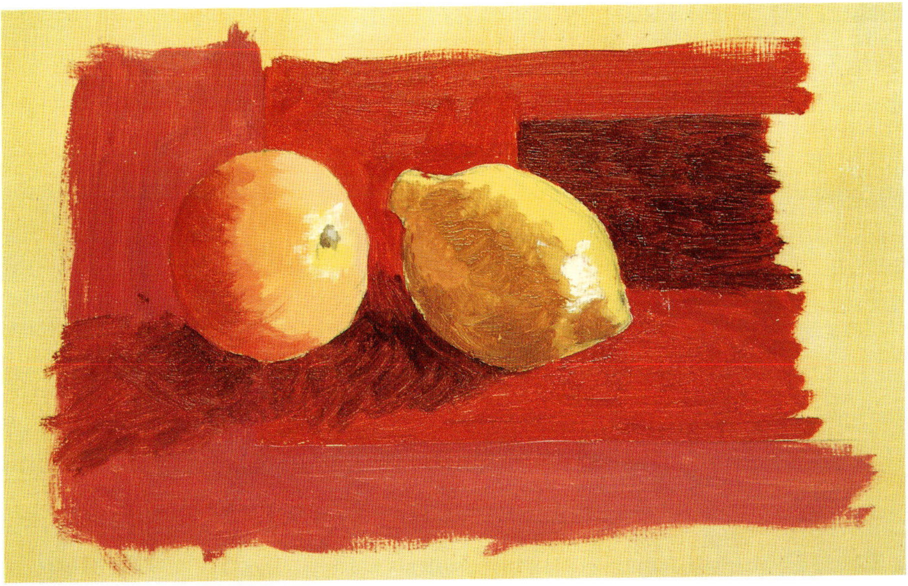

ABOVE

Here I have used the other group of primaries – Winsor (phthalocyanine) blue, alizarin crimson, lemon yellow, and white. Both the lemon and the tablecloth are satisfactory, but the orange is not.

USING SIX COLORS

PAINTING THE same still life group as before, I am now using all six primary colors – ultramarine, Winsor blue, cadmium red, alizarin crimson, cadmium yellow, and lemon yellow – plus white. I am not using black, but producing the darker colors entirely by means of mixtures of the primaries.

1 I begin with the colors of the tablecloth. For this I am using pure alizarin crimson, with white added for the lighter border.

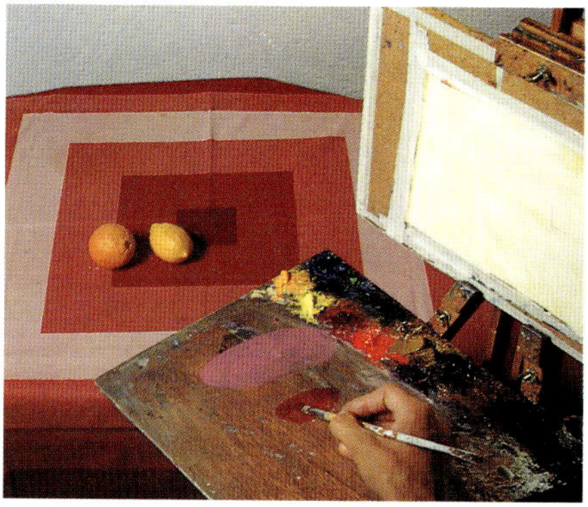

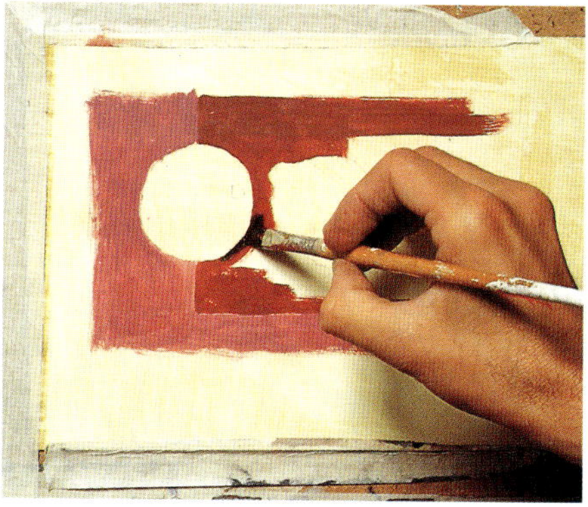

2 By painting the cloth first, I provide myself with a "key" against which I can judge the other colors.

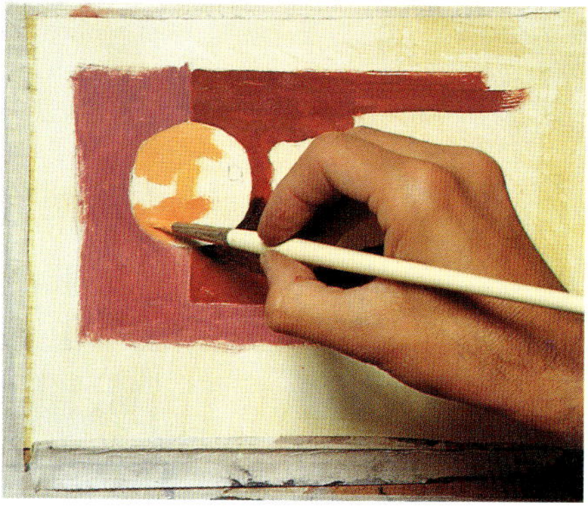

3 For the orange I have begun by using cadmium red and cadmium yellow mixed in different proportions.

4 Having darkened the orange by mixing in a little blue and some alizarin crimson where the color of the cloth is reflected on the fruit, I now set to work on the lemon.

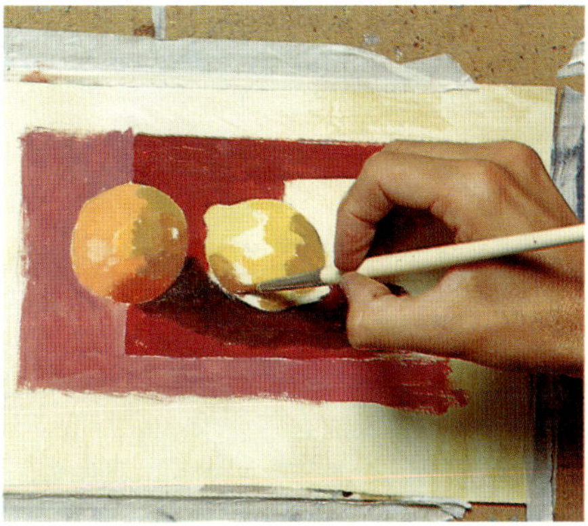

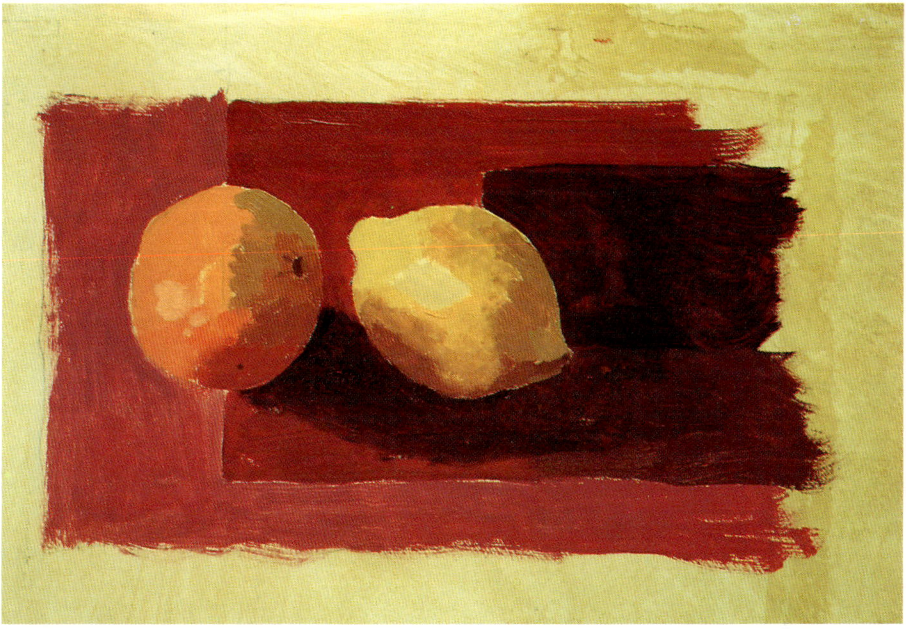

5 For the lighter areas of the lemon I have used lemon yellow and white, while the shadows are brown made from cadmium yellow and alizarin crimson with a tiny touch of blue.

A STARTER PALETTE

THROUGHOUT THIS BOOK I am discussing color as it relates to opaque paints – oils, acrylics, and gouache. The suggested starter palette shown here is for oils, but most acrylic and gouache ranges have similar or identical colors, though the names may be slightly different. Watercolors, too, are made in the same colors, and this palette would form an adequate range for those working in watercolor. Remember, however, that in watercolor white is not added; colors are made lighter by applying them more thinly so that the white of the paper itself shows through.

You may wonder why, when I have just demonstrated the effectiveness of using only six colors, you need any more at all. Although you can make a great many sophisticated mixtures with the primary colors alone, mixing takes time, besides which there are some subjects for which it is helpful to have one or two ready-made greens and browns.

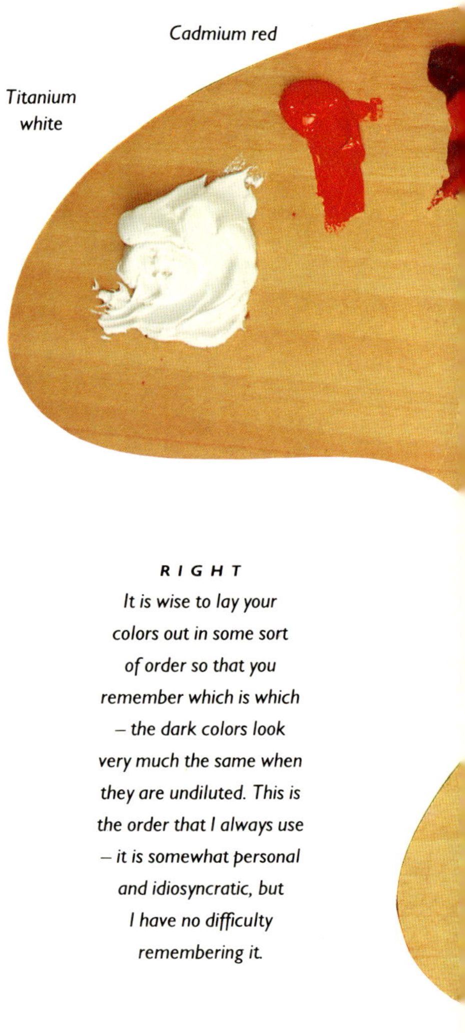

RIGHT
It is wise to lay your colors out in some sort of order so that you remember which is which – the dark colors look very much the same when they are undiluted. This is the order that I always use – it is somewhat personal and idiosyncratic, but I have no difficulty remembering it.

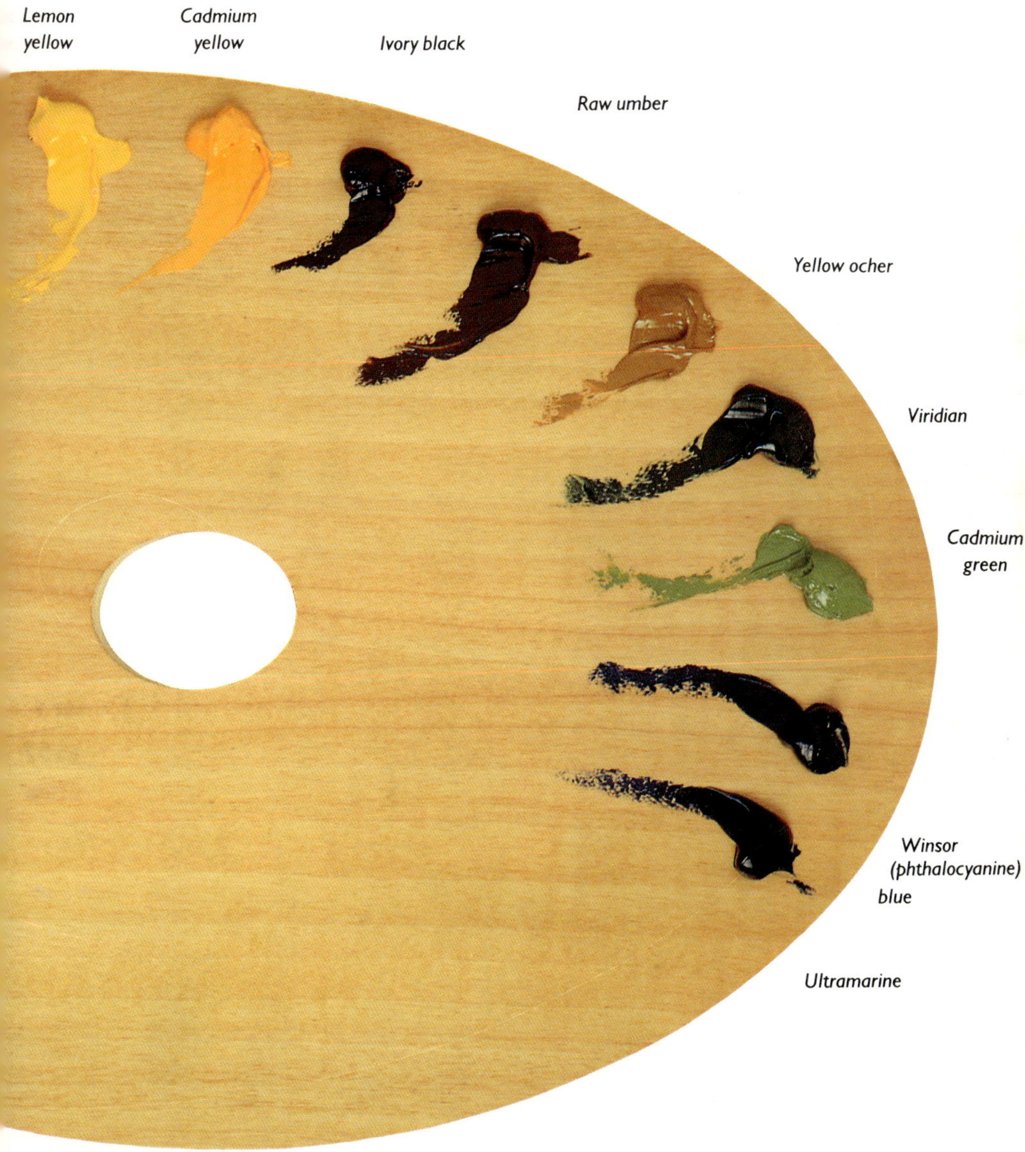
Lemon yellow
Cadmium yellow
Ivory black
Raw umber
Yellow ocher
Viridian
Cadmium green
Winsor (phthalocyanine) blue
Ultramarine

THE STARTER PALETTE IN ACTION

FOR THIS PAINTING I have used only the colors shown on pages 18–19. I seldom depart from this palette, except when painting subjects such as flowers, when I may add one or two colors that are particularly difficult to mix. Some of these are shown on pages 44–7.

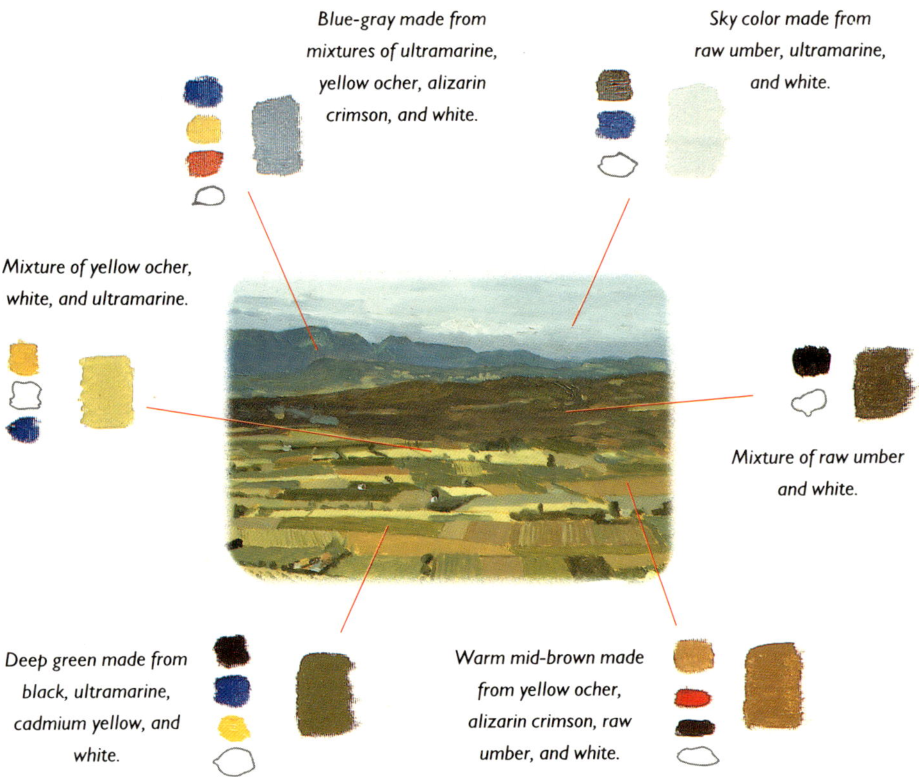

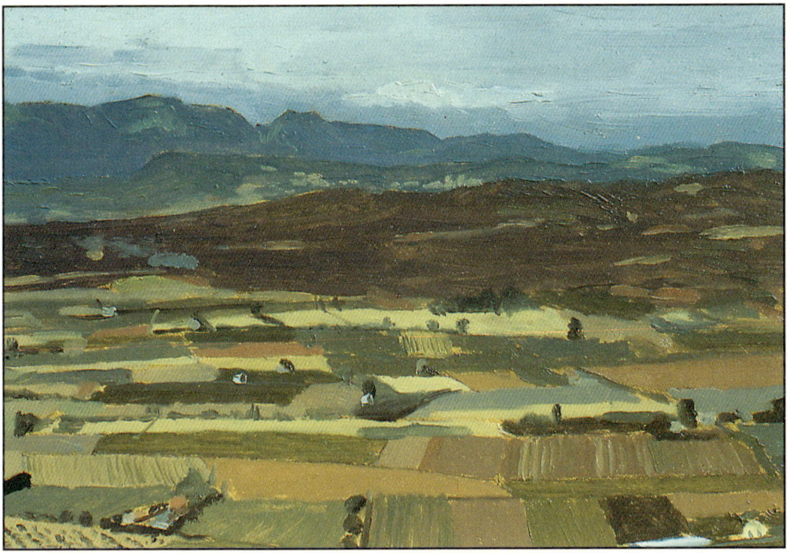

ABOVE AND OPPOSITE

It is best to stick to a familiar range of colors, as you will quickly discover which ones produce the mixtures you want. If you frequently change, you will be dealing with unknown quantities in terms of color, which can lead to mistakes and wasted paint. The color swatches opposite show some of the mixtures used in this painting.

MIXING GREENS

IF YOU ARE interested in painting landscape, as I am, you will certainly have noticed the incredible range of greens you see, particularly in early summer. There are blue-greens, brilliant yellow-greens, deep, rich olive greens, and greens bordering on brown. All artists have their own favorite mixtures for greens, and you will probably discover one or two of your own, but you might like to try some of the mixtures here.

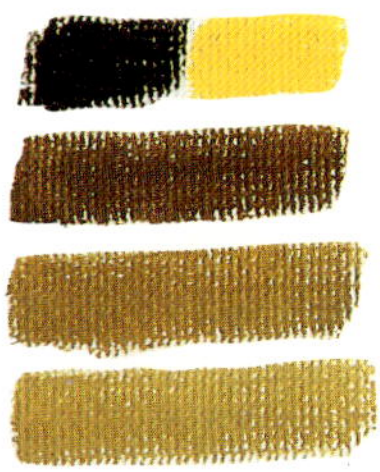

Black and lemon yellow.

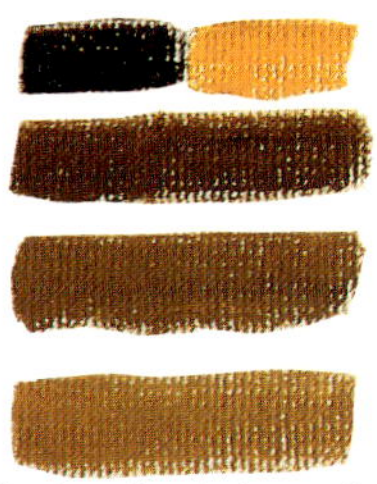

Black and cadmium yellow.

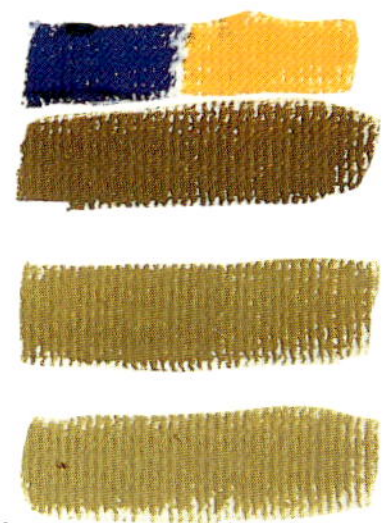

Ultramarine and cadmium yellow.

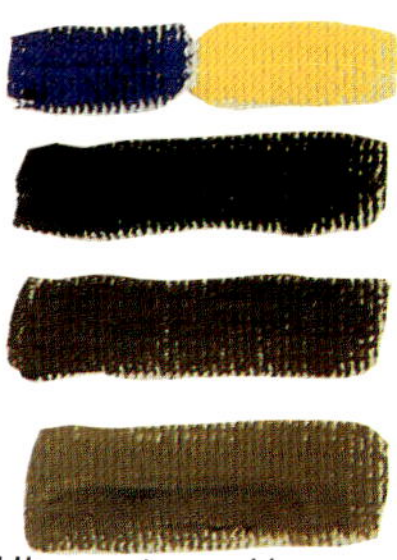

Ultramarine and lemon yellow.

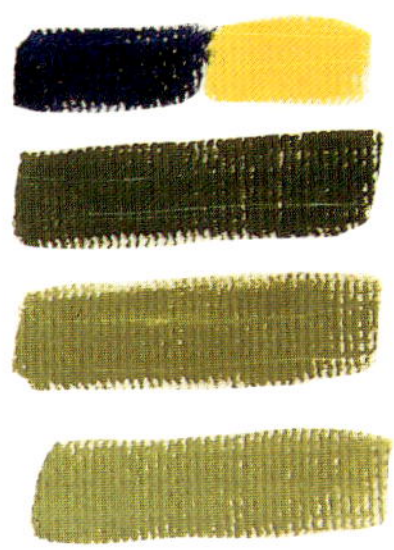

Winsor (phthalocyanine) blue and lemon yellow.

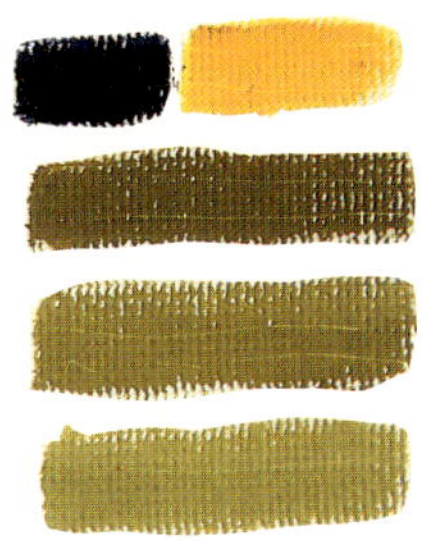

Winsor blue and cadmium yellow.

ABOVE AND OPPOSITE

These charts show first the two colors that produce the mixture, then a "straight," approximately 50/50 mix, and then the mixed color diluted with varying amounts of white.

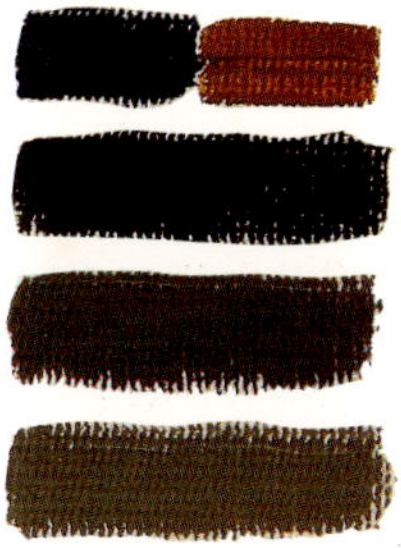

Winsor blue and yellow ocher.

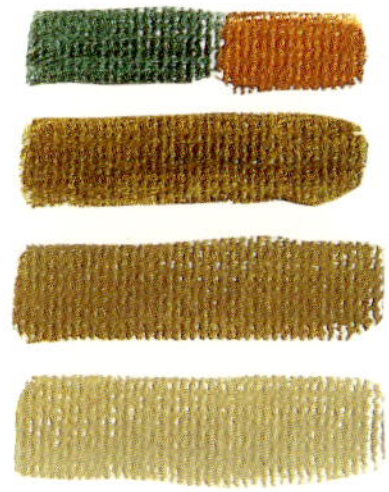

Viridian and yellow ocher.

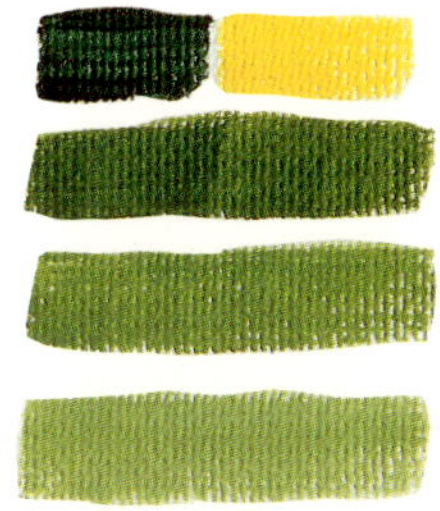

Viridian and lemon yellow.

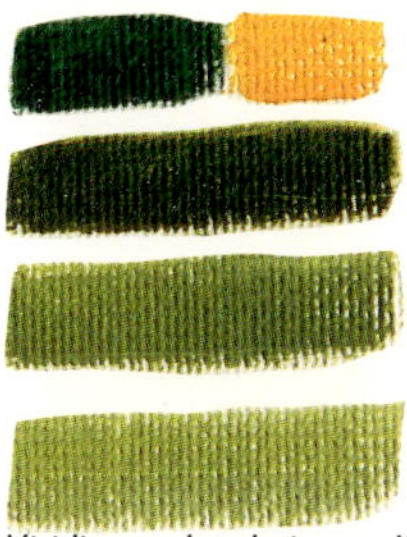

Viridian and cadmium yellow.

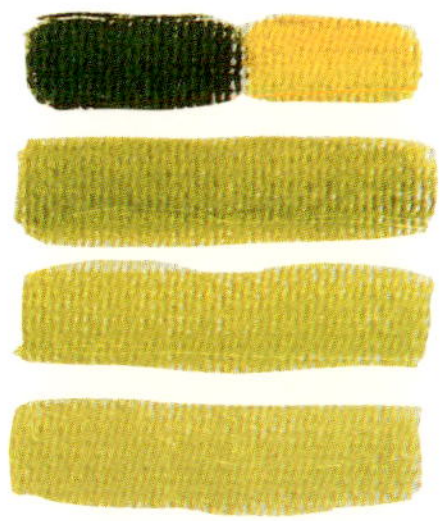

Cadmium green and lemon yellow.

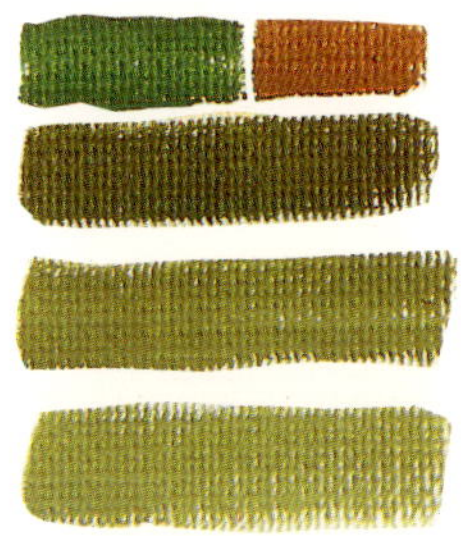

Cadmium green and yellow ocher.

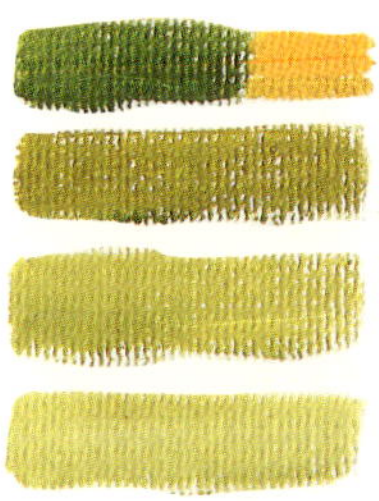

Cadmium green and cadmium yellow.

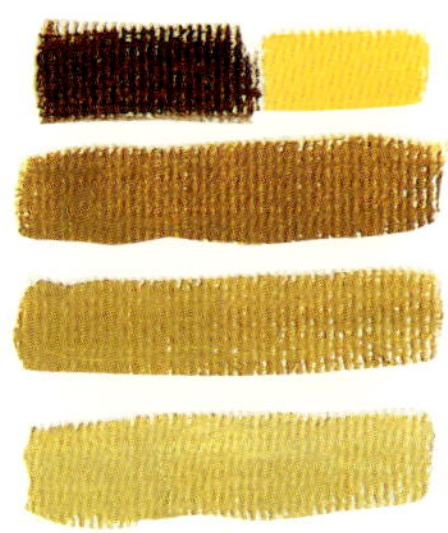

Raw umber and lemon yellow.

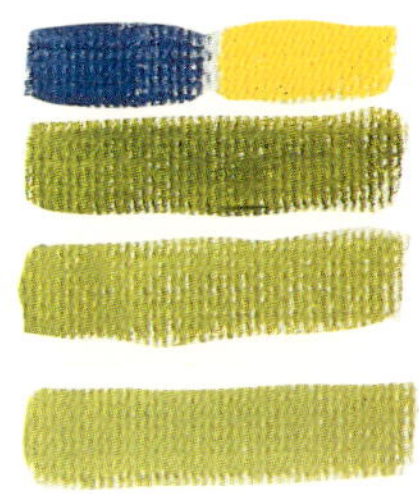

Cerulean blue and lemon yellow.

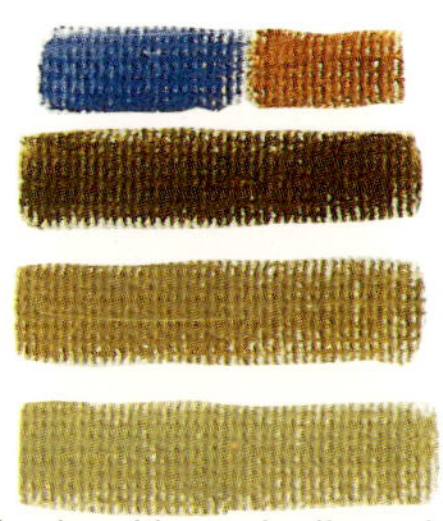

Cerulean blue and yellow ocher.

MIXING BROWNS

BROWNS, LIKE GREENS, are very varied, ranging from colors that might be described as yellow to red-browns, green-browns, and near purples. Raw umber, the only brown in the starter palette, is a useful color, but it will not cover all eventualities, so try out some of the mixtures suggested here and see whether you can come up with some of your own.

Two-color mixtures

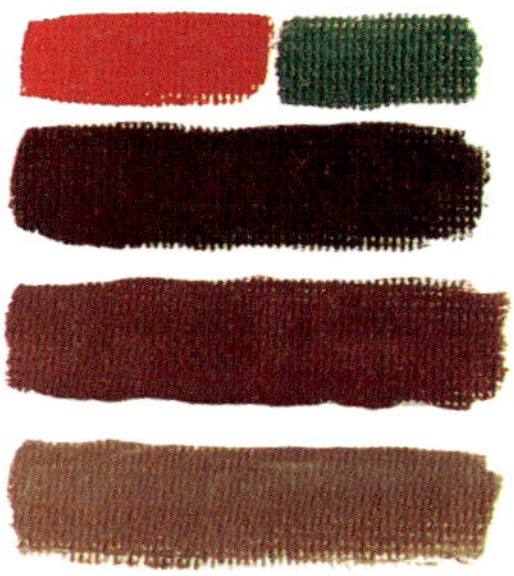

Cadmium red and cadmium green.

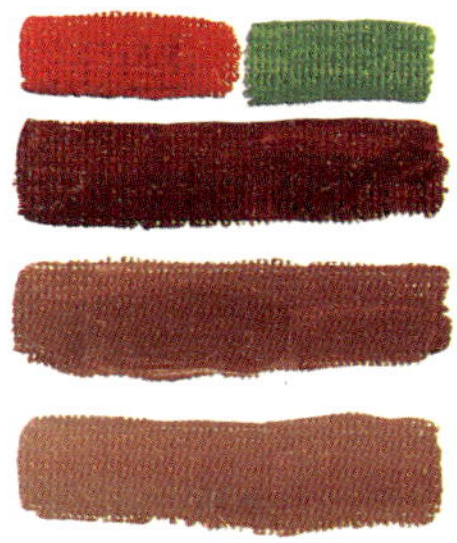

Alizarin crimson and cadmium green.

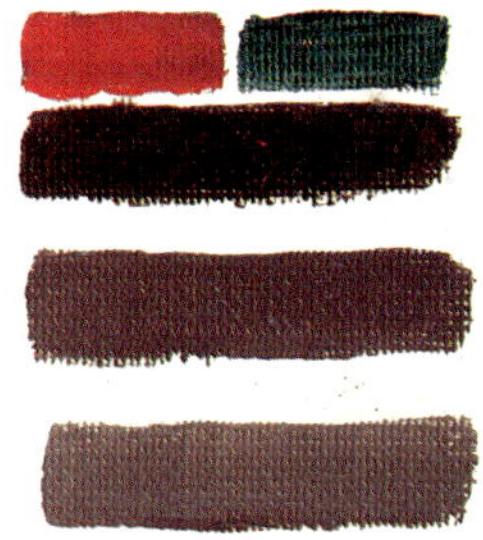

Cadmium red and viridian.

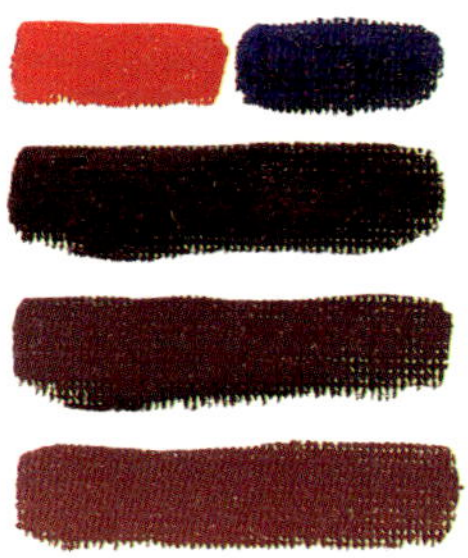

Cadmium red and ultramarine.

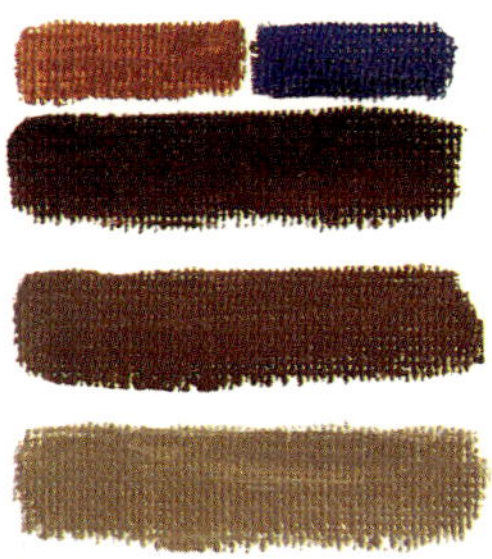

Yellow ocher and ultramarine.

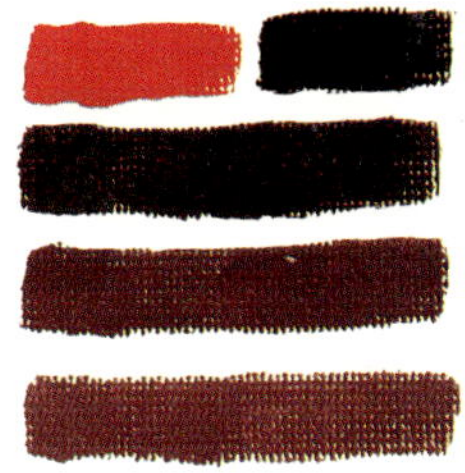

Cadmium red and black.

ABOVE AND OPPOSITE

The first three two-color mixtures (top) have been made by combining two complementary colors – red and green. The second row (above) shows other two-color mixtures, while the opposite page gives some suggestions for three-color mixtures.

Three-color mixtures

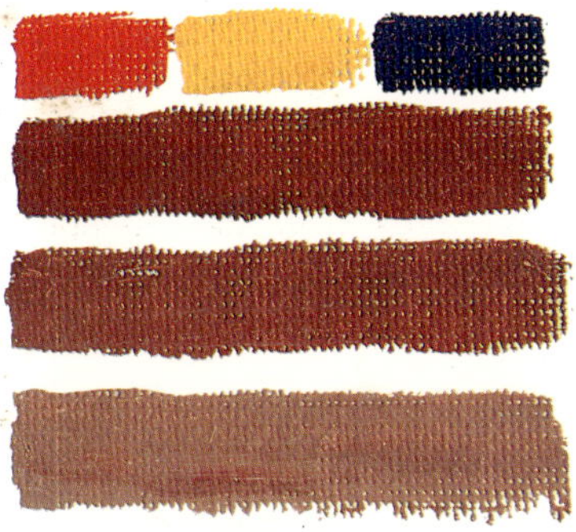

Cadmium red, cadmium yellow, and ultramarine.

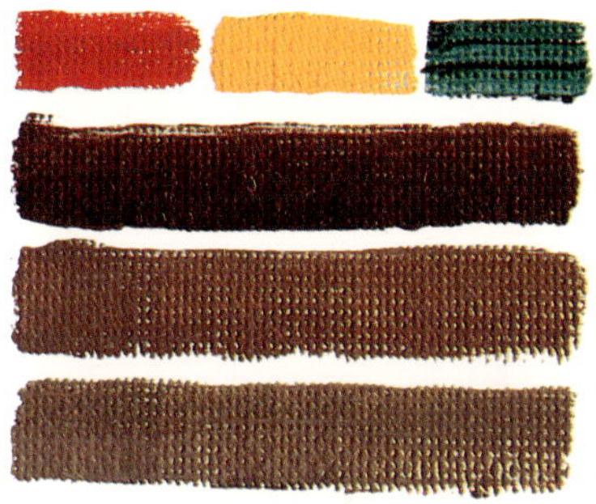

Cadmium red, cadmium yellow, and viridian.

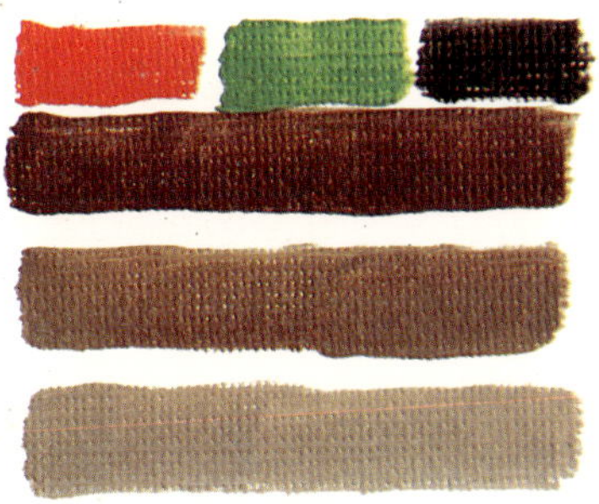

Cadmium red, cadmium green, and black.

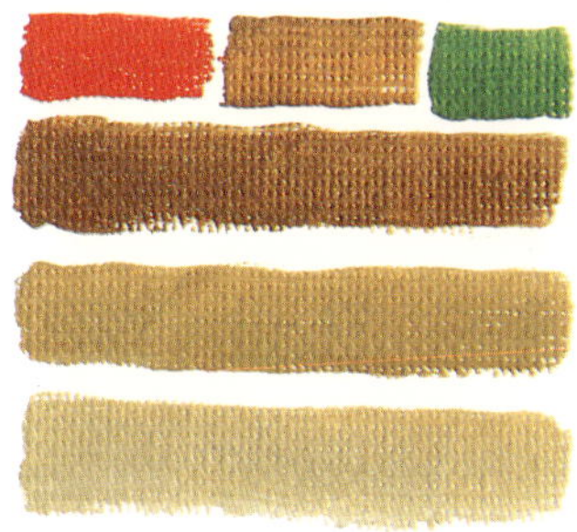

Cadmium red, yellow ocher, and cadmium green.

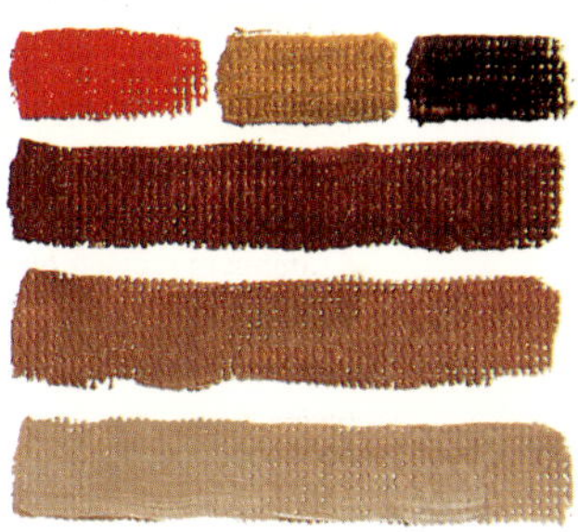

Alizarin crimson, yellow ocher, and raw umber.

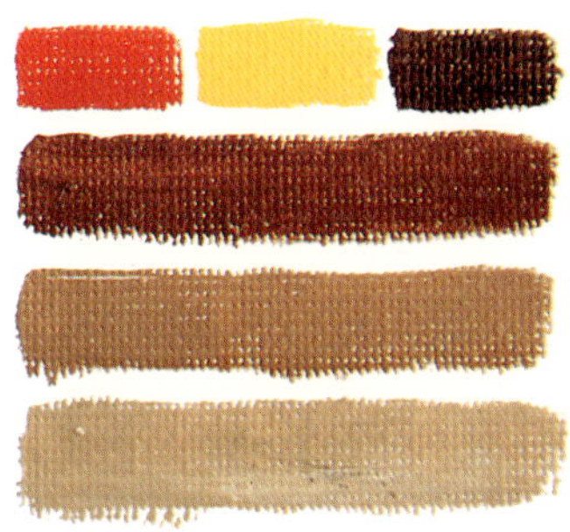

Cadmium red, lemon yellow, and raw umber.

THE COLOR WHEEL

YOU CAN PAINT perfectly well without knowing anything about color theory, but some knowledge of the characteristics of colors can save you a lot of trial and error. Making color wheels like the one shown here will help you to understand how colors relate to each other. Two important concepts in painting are those of harmony and contrast. If you use colors close to one another on the wheel you will create harmonious effects, while colors that are opposite one another give strong contrasts.

Something else you will find it useful to know is that some colors are perceived as "cool" and others as "warm." The oranges, reds and yellows, grouped on one side of the wheel, are the warm ones, while the blues, greens, and purples on the other side are cool. The warm colors tend to "advance" to the front of the picture, while the cool colors push themselves back. This is important because using warm/cool contrasts helps you to describe space in a painting. In a landscape, for example, you can create a sense of depth by using cool colors in the background and warm ones in the foreground. This effect is demonstrated on pages 30–1, and there is more about warm and cool colors on pages 28–9.

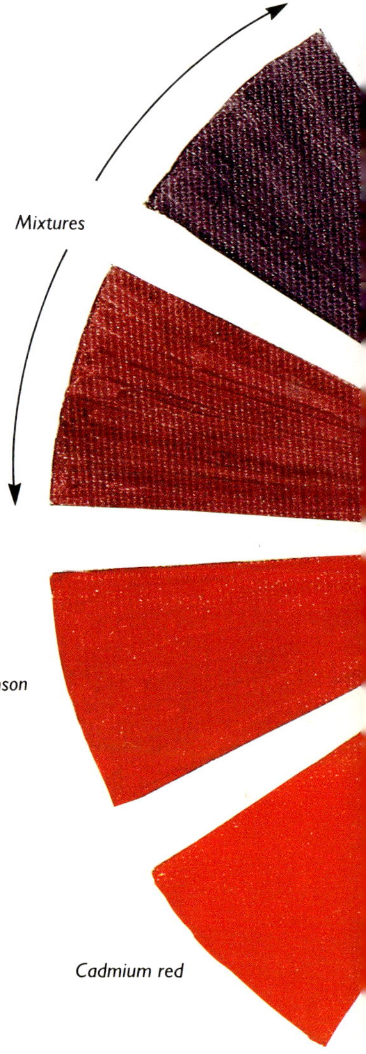

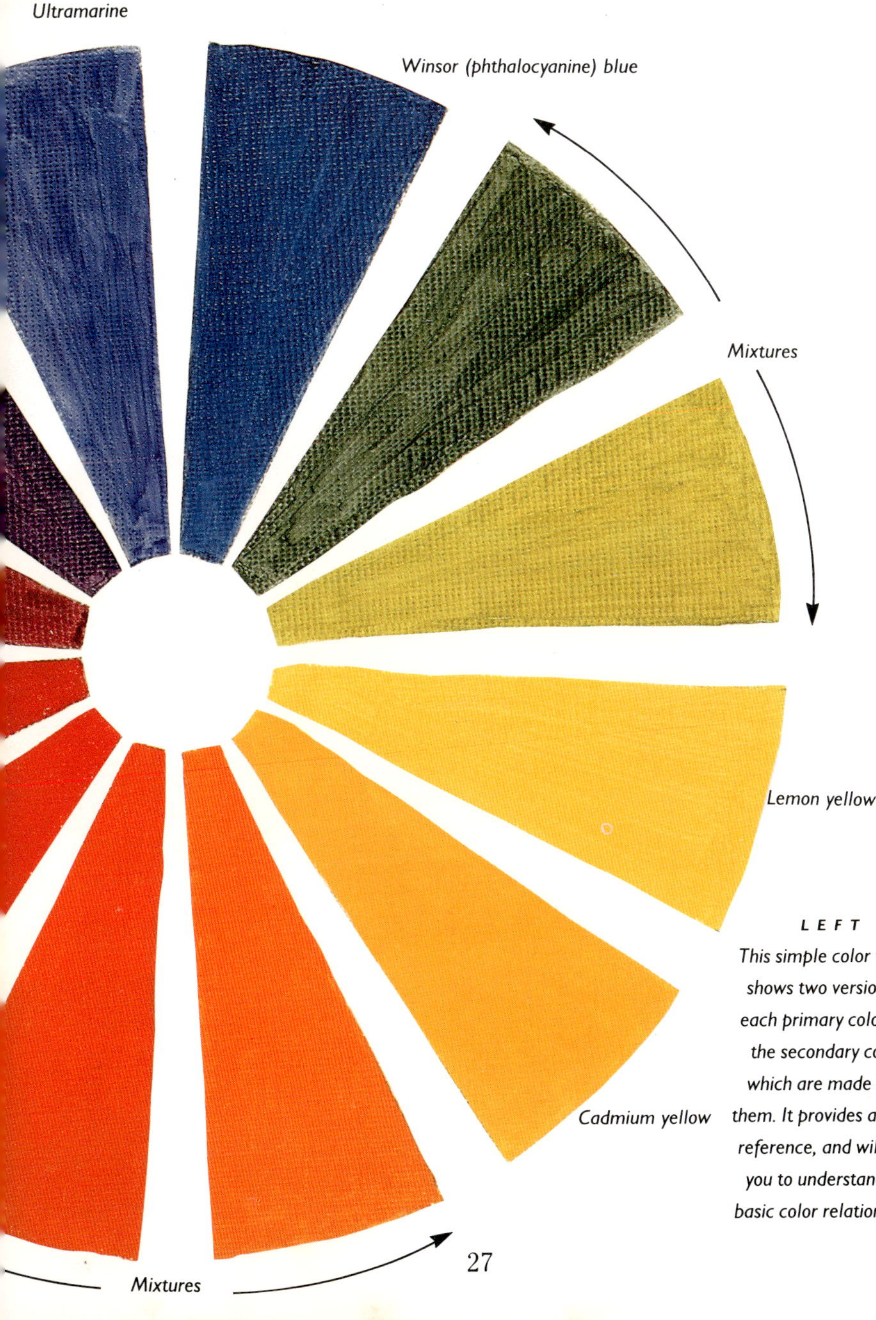

LEFT
This simple color wheel shows two versions of each primary color and the secondary colors which are made from them. It provides a useful reference, and will help you to understand the basic color relationships.

WARM AND COOL COLORS

THE CONCEPT OF warm and cool colors is not quite as simple as it sounds because most colors have warm and cool versions. Look at the two blues shown here, and you will see that one is slightly green (cool) and the other slightly red (warm). Greens vary from very cool when they have a high blue content, to distinctly warm when there is more yellow. Even red has warm and cool versions. Alizarin crimson, for instance, is cool when placed next to cadmium red, but if you were to juxtapose it with a really cool color, such as a blue-gray, it would then appear warm.

The single most important fact to realize about colors is that none of them exists in isolation – each color is "made" by the way it plays against other colors. Paint an area of bright orange and surround it with gray and it will hit you in the eye, but, if you surround the same orange with red of a similar intensity, the impact will be made by the two colors together.

ABOVE

Alizarin crimson trying to recede, but not doing so because it lies over the cadmium red.

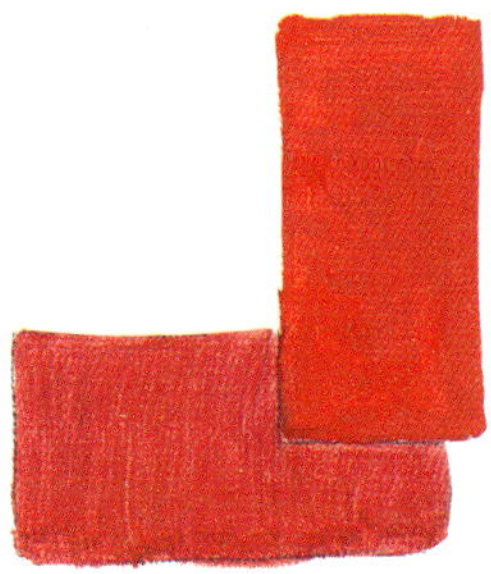

ABOVE

Here cadmium red advances not only because it is warmer than the alizarin crimson, but because it is used more thickly.

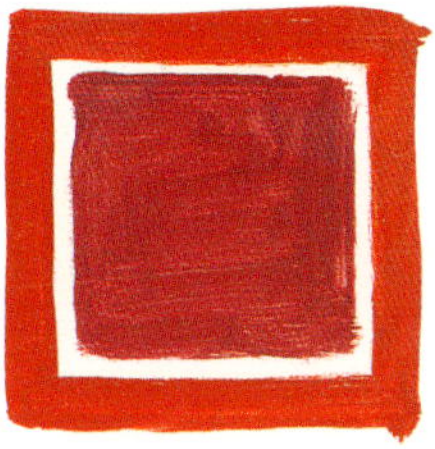

ABOVE
Alizarin crimson, cooled with a touch of white, in a border of cadmium red (warm).

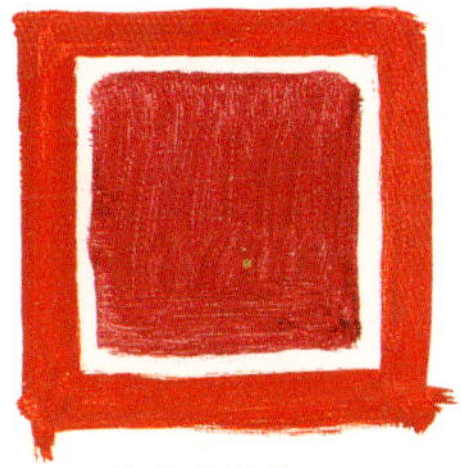

ABOVE
Pure alizarin crimson in a border of cadmium red.

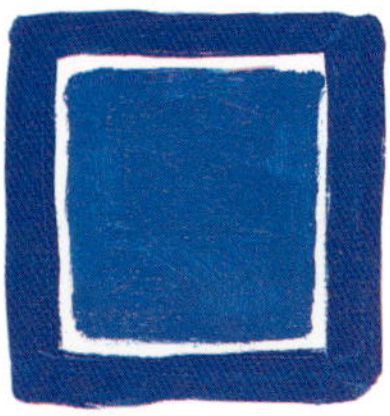

ABOVE
Winsor (phthalocyanine) blue (cool) in a border of ultramarine (warm). A little white has been added to both colors.

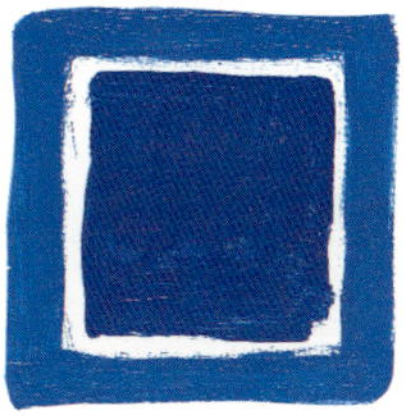

ABOVE
Ultramarine in a border of Winsor (phthalocyanine) blue. A little white has again been added.

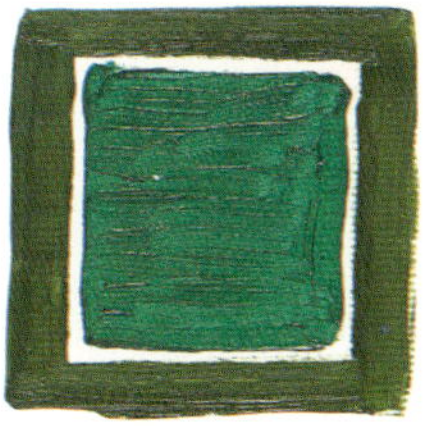

ABOVE
Viridian is a very cool blue-green. Here it is seen surrounded by cadmium green, which is warm (yellowish).

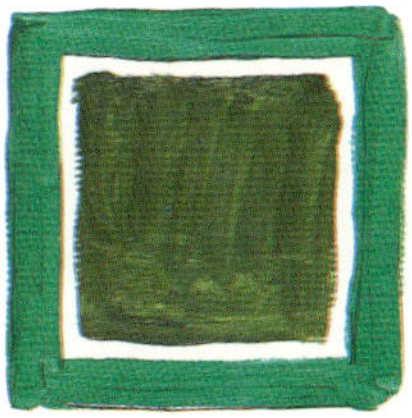

ABOVE
The cadmium green, now in the center, pushes forward, away from the viridian. These warm/cool contrasts are more obvious than those of the blues.

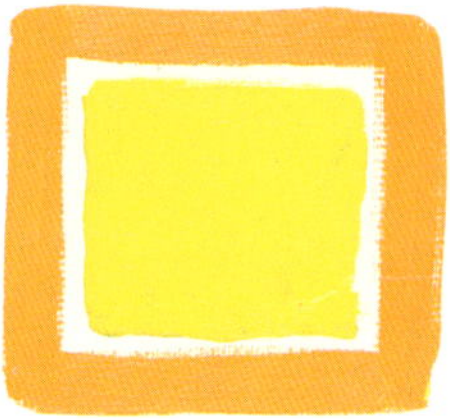

ABOVE
The warm/cool contrasts are also marked in the yellows. Lemon yellow, a cool acid color, is here surrounded by cadmium yellow, warm and orangey.

USING WARM AND COOL CONTRASTS

THIS PHOTOGRAPH provides a good example of the concept of color temperature. Because the tree in the middle ground is the warmest as well as the most vivid color, it seems to push itself forwards to the front of the picture, with the foreground shrinking back.

However, what is interesting in a photograph – or in reality – does not always make a good painting, so here I have set out to alter the balance, introducing warmer colors into the foreground to force the tree back into its natural position in space.

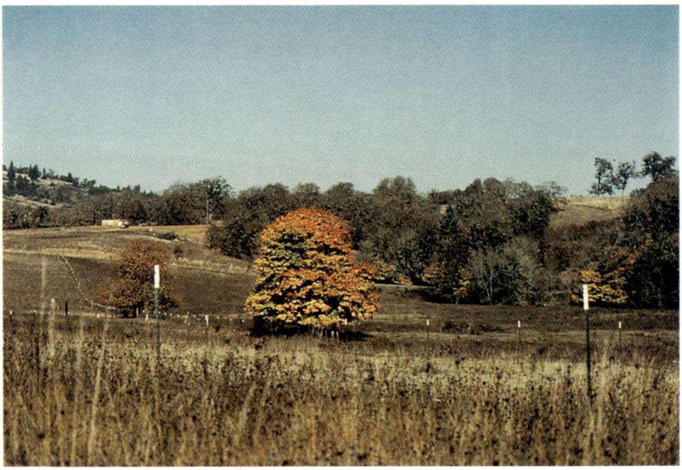

ABOVE

The tree seems to push forwards to the front of the photograph because it is the warmest and brightest color.

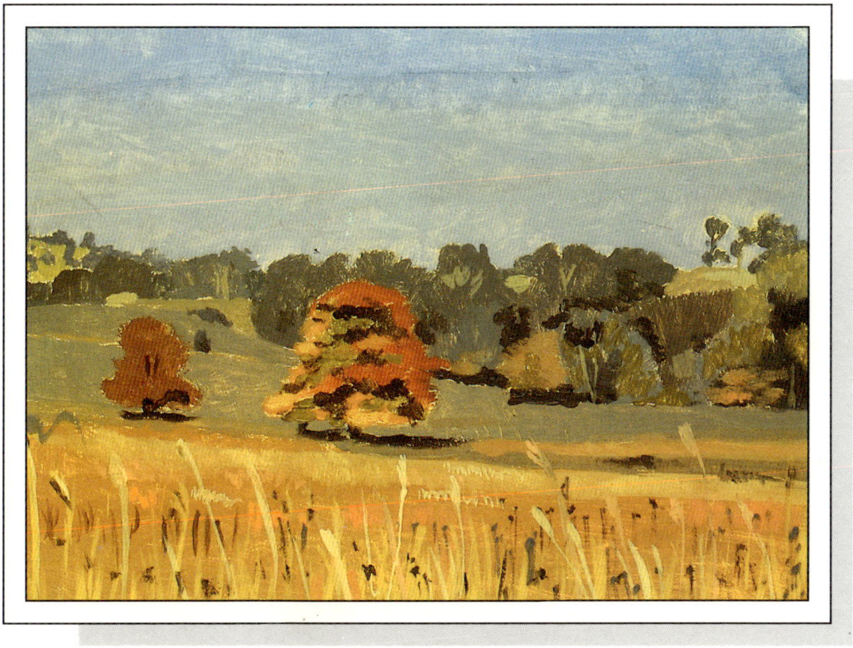

ABOVE

In the painting, the tree no longer dominates. As well as using warmer colors in the foreground, more detail is added than is seen in the photograph, which helps to bring the area into focus.

Complementary Colors

These are the colors that lie opposite to one another on the color wheel (see pages 26–7) – red and green, yellow and violet, blue and orange. They are important in painting because they allow you to set up particularly vibrant contrasts. Add small touches of red to a landscape, for example, and you heighten the green and give the whole picture an extra sparkle.

The red/green combination is frequently used in landscape and flower painting, since these colors are often present in nature, which is itself rich in complementary contrasts. You can exaggerate what you see to introduce complementary colors. The Impressionists claimed that they could always see touches of any object's complementary color in the shadow – a yellow building, for example, with violet shadows. They used complementaries extensively in their work, as do many of today's artists.

Another interesting thing about these colors is that when you mix them together they "neutralize" each other, producing an interesting range of grays and browns. Some of these are shown on pages 24–5 and 40–1.

RIGHT
Here I have used red with a slightly muted version of its complementary – green.

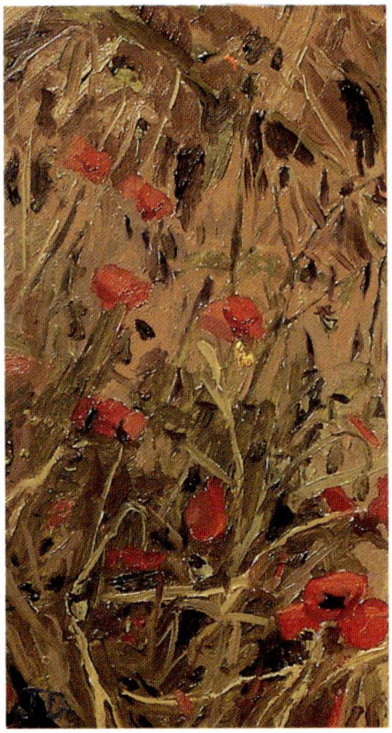

OPPOSITE
Flowers provide a good opportunity to use complementary contrasts. Here the yellow/violet dominates, but the other pairs of complementaries are present also.

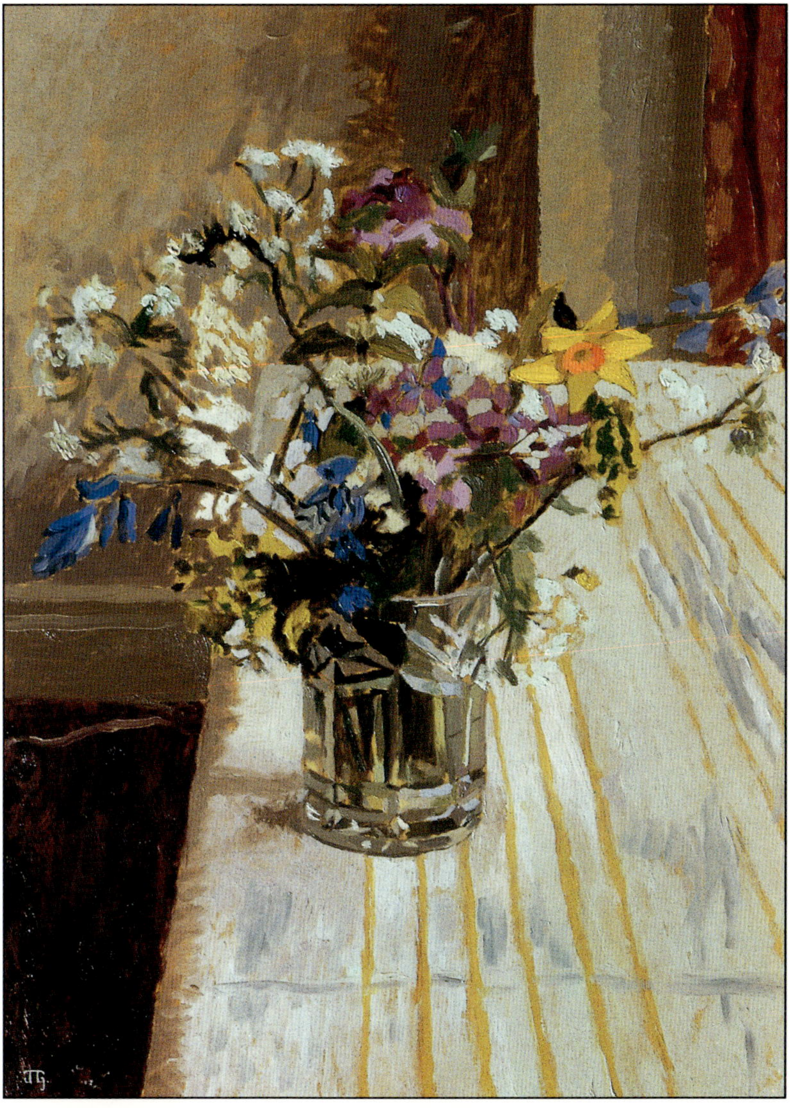

COLOR AND TONE

THE WORD TONE refers to the lightness or darkness of a color, and it is important for two reasons. First, it is tone that models form – the way the light strikes an object, creating highlights and shaded areas, defines its roundness or angularity. Second, a painting needs to have a good balance of lights and darks, because it will look bland and dull without these tonal contrasts.

It is surprisingly difficult to judge the tones of colors because our eyes always register colors first. We can see immediately that something is green, blue or orange, but it takes more thought and observation to work out how dark or light it is in relation to its surroundings. Skies are a particular problem. Even when a sky appears a vivid blue, it will usually (though not always) be lighter than a tree or hill below or in front of it since the sky is the source of light. You will find it easier to judge tones if you half-close your eyes, which reduces the impact of the colors and cuts out distracting detail.

Another way of seeing colors and tones in a landscape is to view it sideways or upside down. The unexpected immediately becomes apparent.

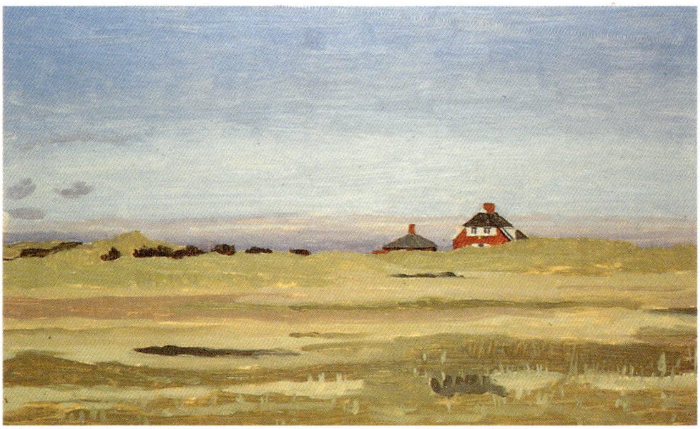

ABOVE

The sky and land are almost the same tone in this painting.

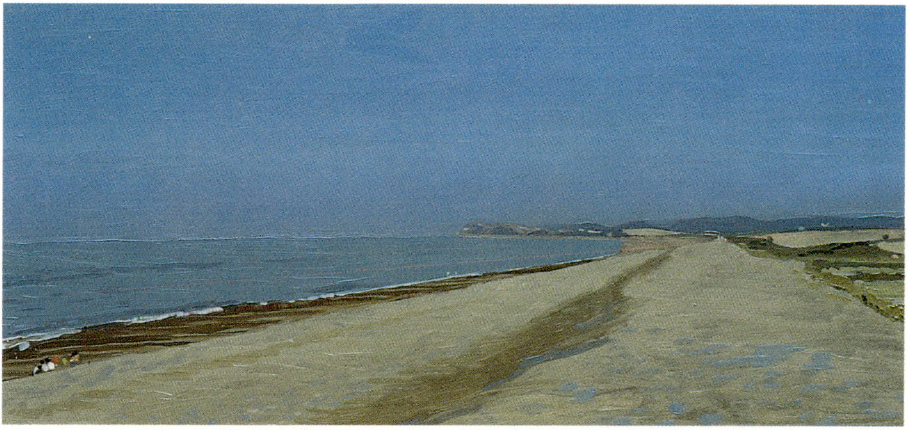

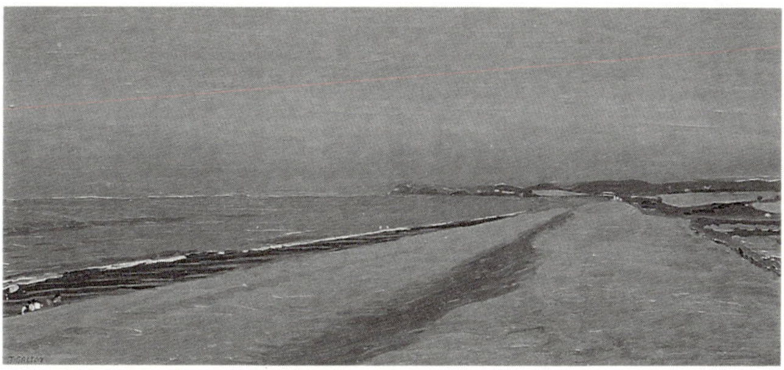

ABOVE

It was equally difficult to assess the tones here, as the contrast between land and sky was very small. The black and white photograph gives a clearer picture.

ANALYZING TONE

YOU MAY FIND it useful to carry out some exercises to help you analyze tone, working entirely in monochrome as I have done in these two examples. You do not have to choose a landscape; you can set up a simple still life or draw a person, if you prefer. Make one drawing in pencil or charcoal, looking carefully at your subject to decide which are the darkest and which the lightest tones.

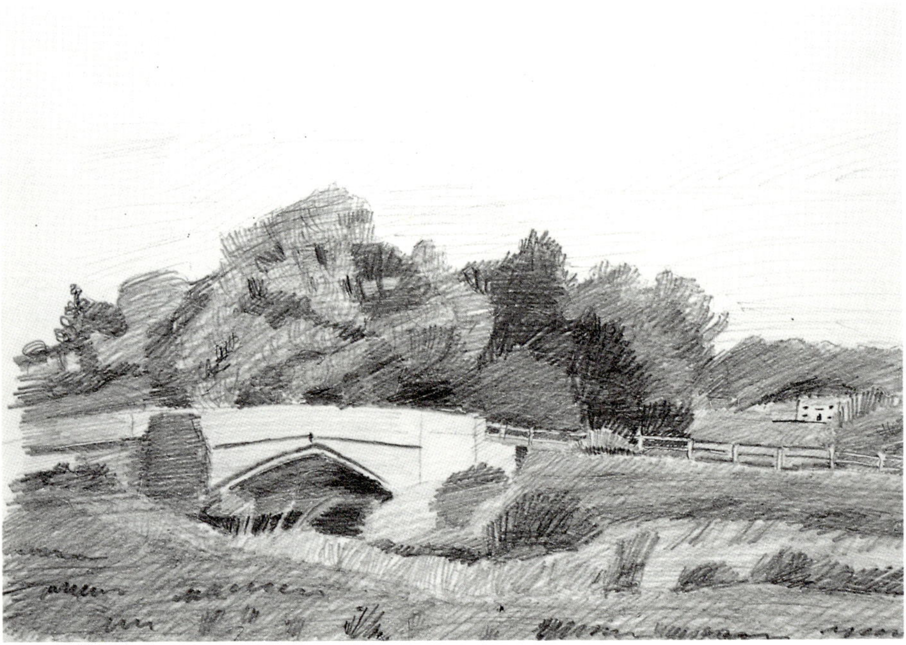

ABOVE

Soft pencil is ideal for making tonal studies. Try to identify the main light and dark tones first, or your drawing will become confused.

Then try working in opaque paint – oil, acrylic, or gouache – putting down the darkest tones first, and then working up through the middle ranges to the highlights. When you have finished, you may find that you have made the dark tones too dark, which is a common error. Dark colors often seem black when you first look at them, but they are not – there are no true blacks in nature.

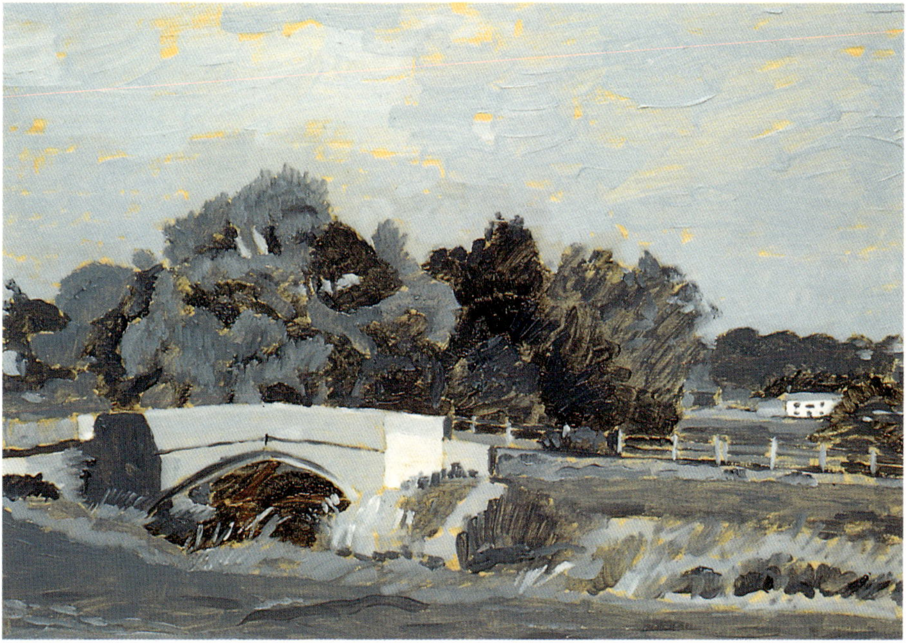

ABOVE

Here I have made a monochrome study in oil paint, with the yellow-brown of the board showing through the paint in places to give a hint of color.

Color and Light

WITHOUT LIGHT, colors could not exist. This much is obvious, but it is more difficult to accept the degree to which light – and shade – changes "local" colors. The local color of an object is its actual color – a lemon is yellow, grass is green, and so on. However, when you look closely at a lemon you will see that very little of it is actually pure lemon yellow. There will be dark areas on the shadowed side that may be greenish, or even quite dark green-brown, while the highlights may be almost pure white, depending on the

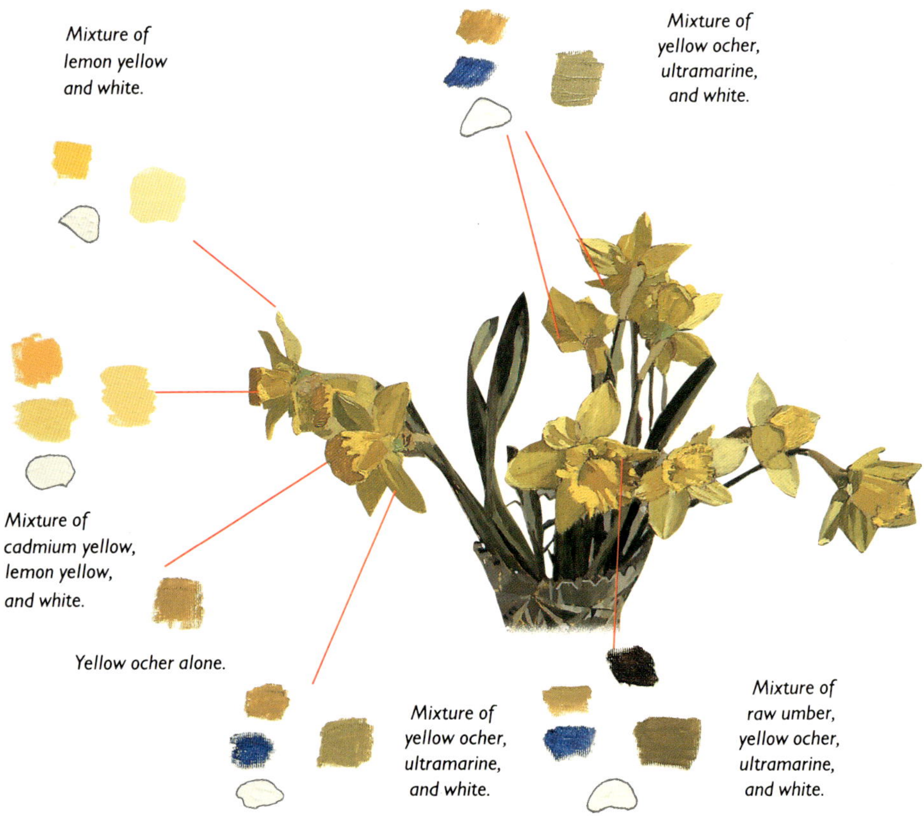

strength of the light. There will be patches of the object's local color, certainly, but often surprisingly few.

Newcomers to painting often find it difficult to believe their own eyes, and therefore fail to identify these color shifts. You know an object is a certain color, and think that by painting it more or less the same all over, with perhaps some tentative brown shadows, you can make it appear more colorful. But in fact the reverse is true; it will look not only flat but also less colorful since there is no contrast.

One of the joys of painting is manipulating color, and you will find that you can make an object's local color look more convincing, not less so, by being honest with yourself about the colors you see.

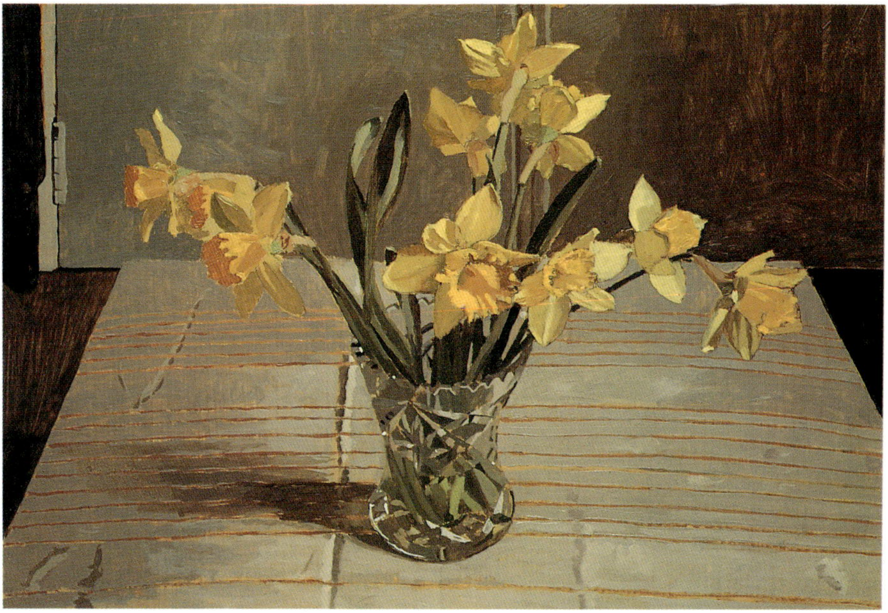

ABOVE AND OPPOSITE

In my painting of daffodils there is no mistaking that the flowers are yellow, though I have used very little pure yellow. The color swatches opposite show some of the mixtures used here.

COLORED GRAYS

GRAYS ARE commonly thought of as a mixture of black and white. These do actually make gray, but it is a dull, uninteresting gray and one that has little to do with reality. Because colors are always modified by the light that falls on them and by the way they are juxtaposed with other colors, even something you know to be a pure black-and-white gray will not look that way when you come to paint it. The so-called "colored grays" are important in painting because they act as a foil for the bright colors, but they must be seen in the context of the other colors in your painting. It is interesting to see how chameleon-like they are, changing according to their surroundings.

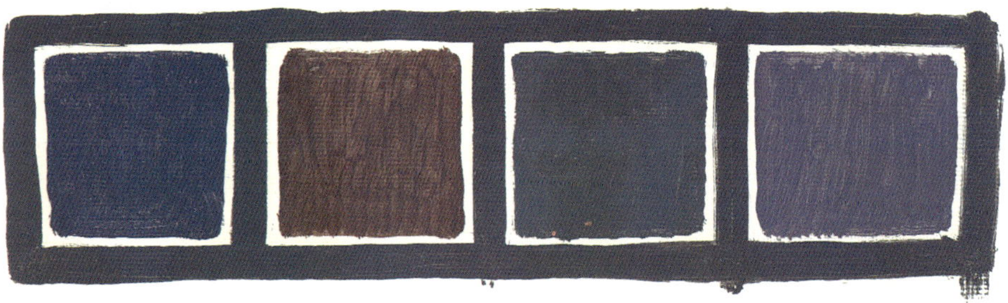

Alizarin crimson and viridian.

Winsor violet and cadmium yellow.

Ultramarine and cadmium red.

Cobalt blue, alizarin crimson and lemon yellow.

ABOVE

These colored grays have been placed in a neutral (black-and-white gray) surround, which makes them look quite vivid. The first two have been made by mixing complementary colors (see pages 32–3).

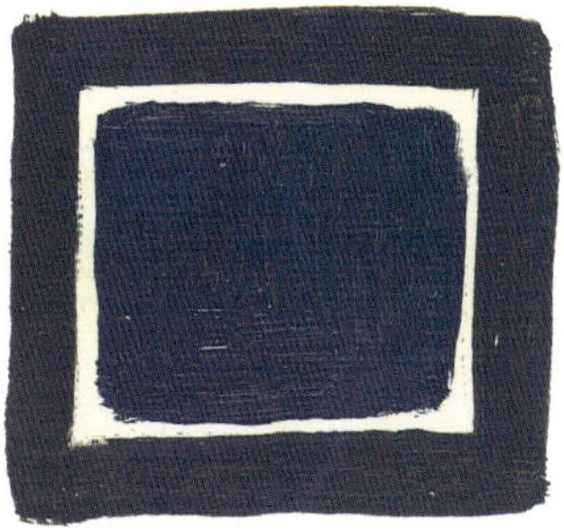

Appears quite mauve.

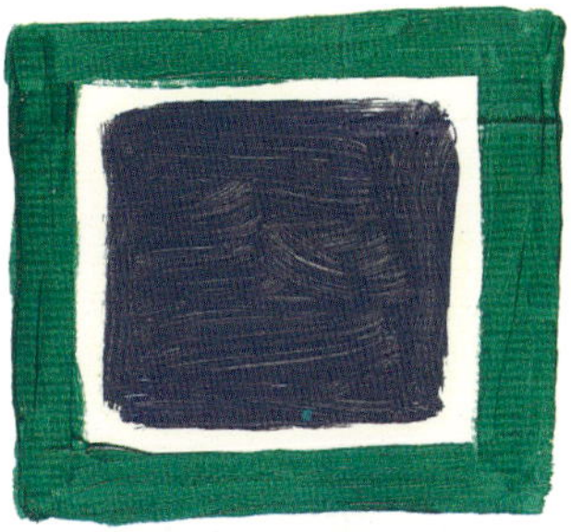

Appears more red.

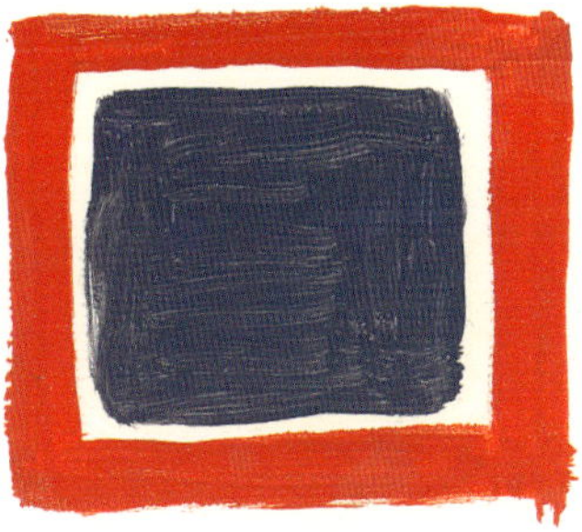

Appears less red.

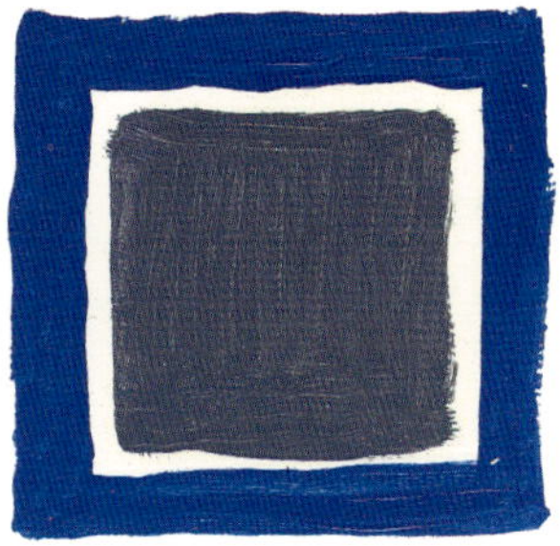

Appears less blue.

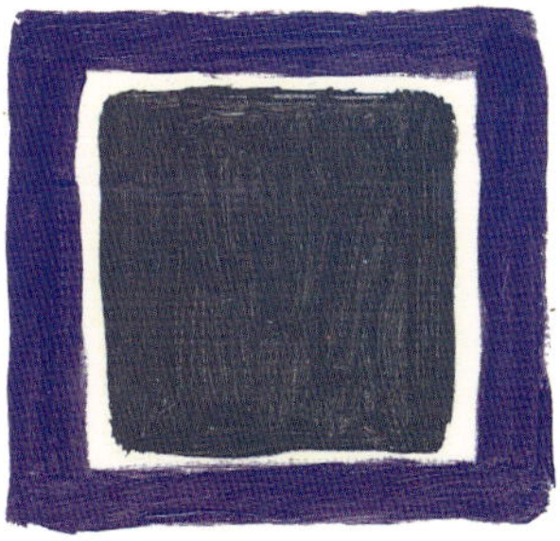

Appears less violet.

LEFT AND ABOVE

Here the first mixture, of alizarin crimson and viridian, has been shown first with a neutral gray border and then surrounded by other colors. Notice how this changes the way it is perceived.

PAINTING WHITE

WHITE AS A description of local color (see pages 38–9) is particularly misleading, because white surfaces are always in reality a subtle mixture of other colors. White reflects light, so it is more obviously influenced by lighting conditions and surroundings than any other color. If you have ever looked at a white house at dusk you may have noticed that it is distinctly blue or mauve, and quite dark in tone. This is an extreme example, of course, but even if you put a white vase in front of a white wall or curtain you will see a fascinating interplay of colored grays and other delicate shades, few of which, except for the occasional bright highlight, are pure white. Similarly, "white" houses, cars, or dogs look dirty against the white of clean snow.

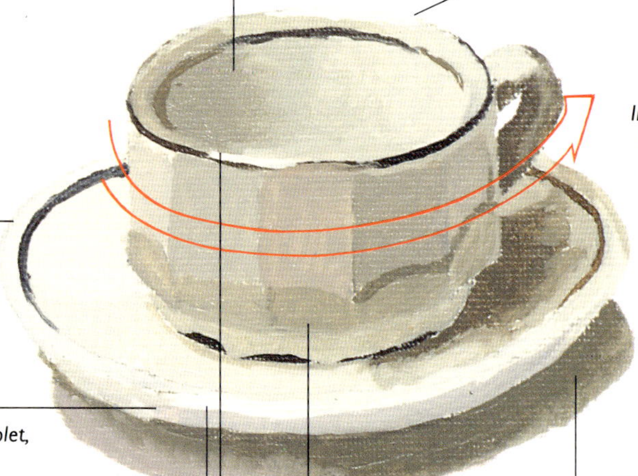

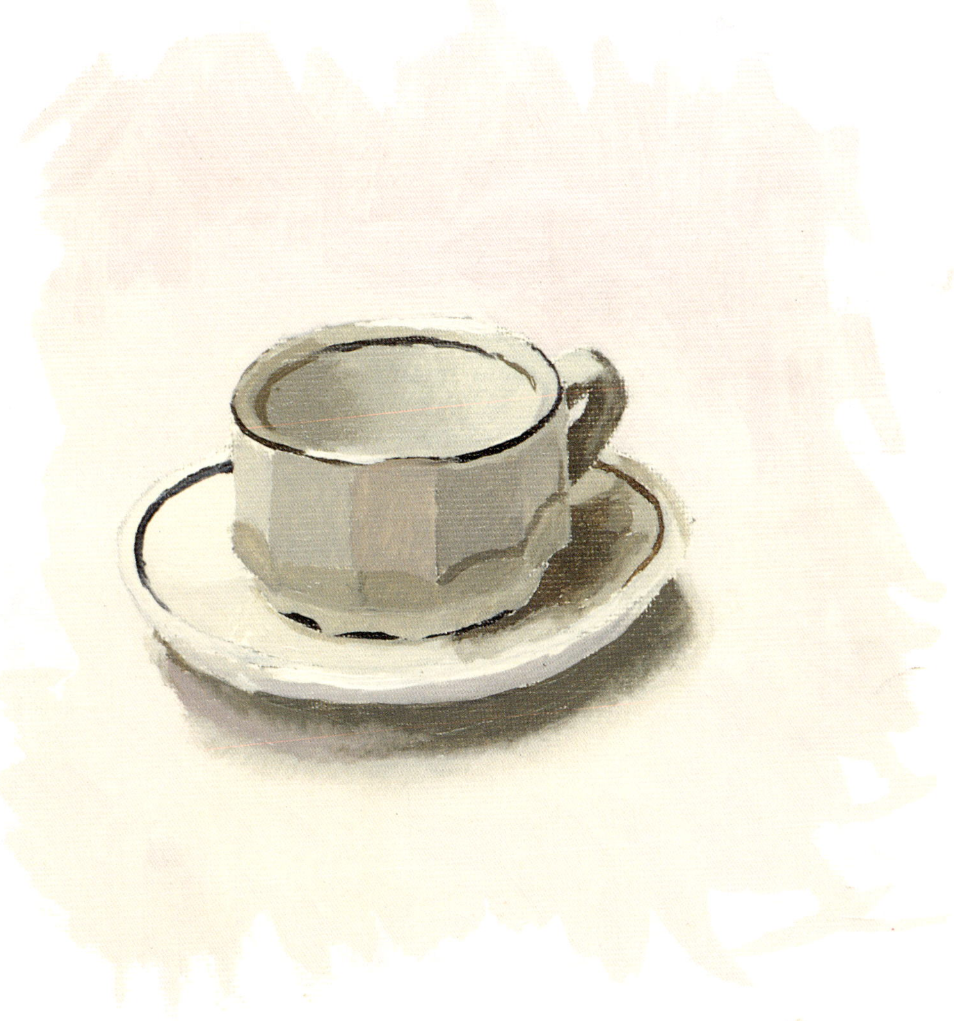

ABOVE

It is worth setting up a simple still life of the kind I have painted here, as it will teach you a lot about analyzing and mixing colors. The color swatches opposite show some of the mixtures used.

DIFFICULT COLORS

HOWEVER SKILLED you are at color mixing, there are always occasions when you will need some special colors. Flowers are a case in point; some of the more vivid shades, such as purples and rose colors, are virtually impossible to mix satisfactorily, while there are some wonderful tube colors that give you a head start. Some of the tube greens, too, are brighter and purer than those you can mix from blues and yellows. You may find that one manufacturer produces a particularly good color, so do not restrict yourself to just one range. Here I have made suggestions for additional colors, and shown the differences between these and mixtures from primary colors.

BELOW
Other bright colors that cannot be mixed.

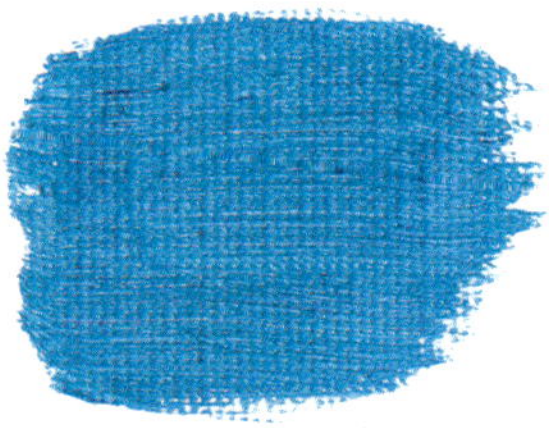

Manganese blue

Cobalt violet

Cadmium scarlet

Rowney rose

Geranium lake

Venetian red

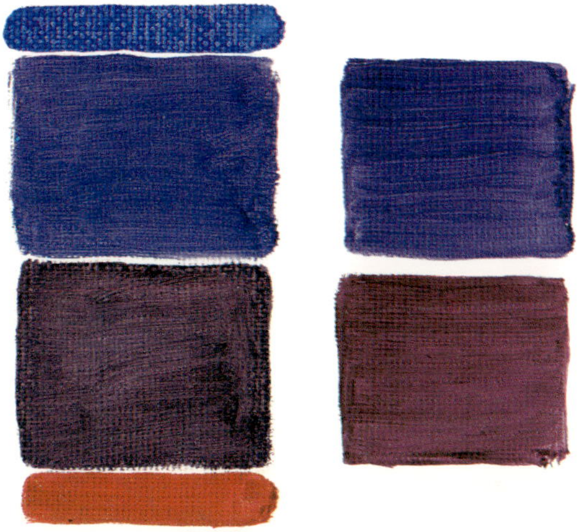

Winsor violet

Magenta

RIGHT
Mixtures of ultramarine and alizarin crimson compared with other purples.

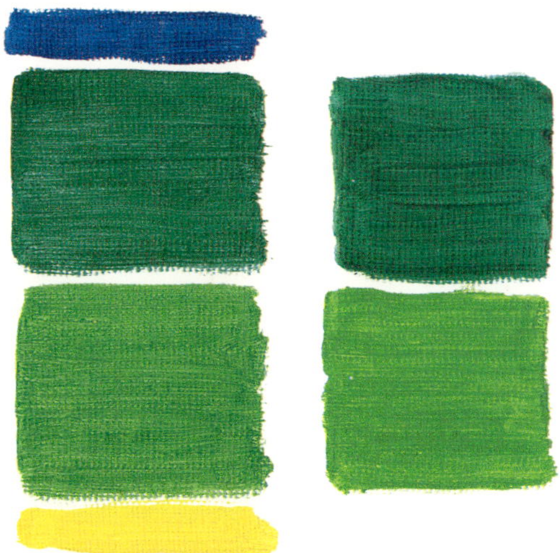

Viridian

Cadmium green

RIGHT
Mixtures of Winsor (phthalocyanine) blue and lemon yellow compared with other greens.

FLOWER COLORS

THE ESSENCE OF flower painting is freshness, so you do not want either to overwork the paint or to overmix the colors. Because I know purples are impossible to mix, I have used Winsor violet extensively, as well as Rowney rose. The violet is a good addition to the starter palette even if you are not painting flowers, since it makes excellent mixes, particularly for skies.

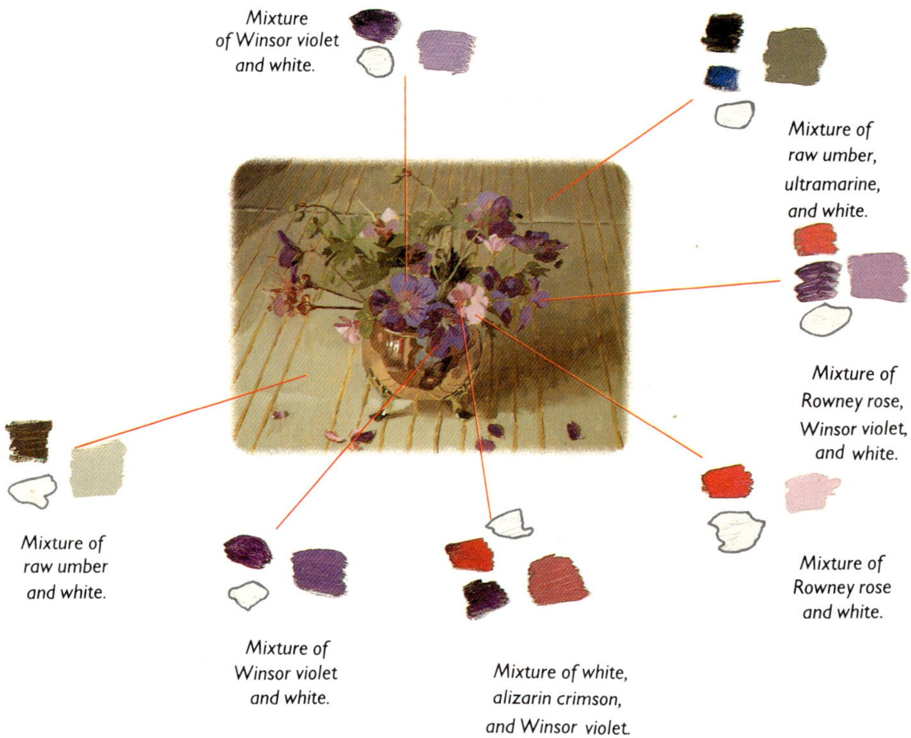

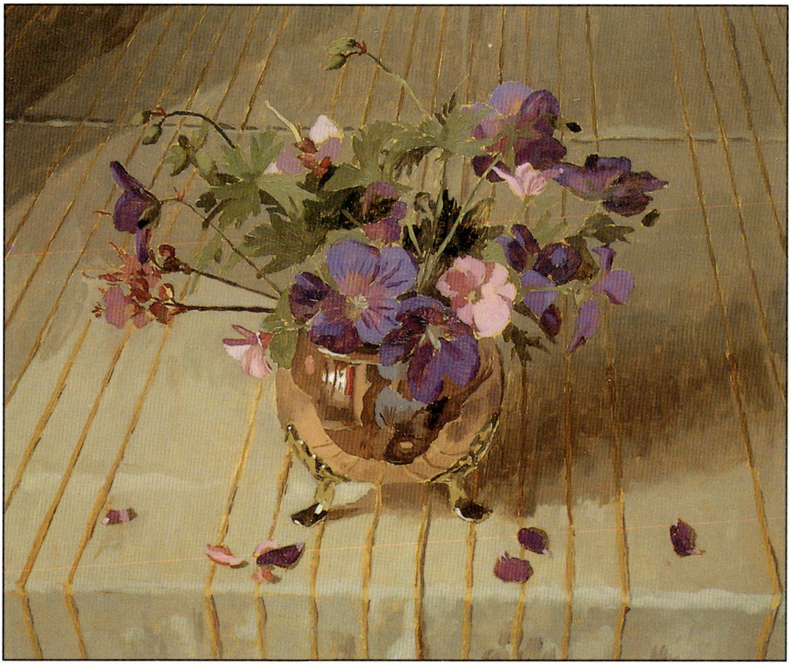

ABOVE AND OPPOSITE

You have to be sure of the capabilities of your colors for flower subjects, since overmixing and overpainting can quickly spoil the freshness of the colors and lead to labored brushwork. The swatches opposite show some of the mixtures used.

Shadow Colors

MANY AMATEUR paintings are spoiled by muddy brown or gray shadows. Shadows certainly can present a problem, as it is not always easy to analyze the colors. Cast shadows are affected by three things: the color of the ground on which the shadow is cast, the color of the object that casts the shadow, and last, but by no means least, the "color" of the light. Most

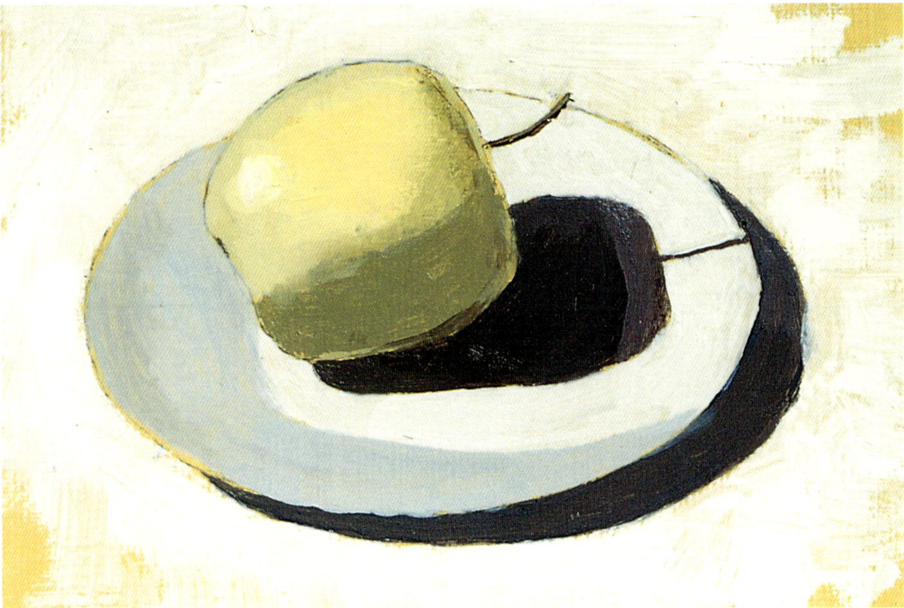

ABOVE

Because I have chosen a white object, the shadows are not confused by the ground color or by any other reflected color. For this study I worked out of doors.

people have probably noticed that shadows often look blue. This is simply because they reflect the color of the sky – shadows are not a total eclipse of light; if they were, they would be black.

The blueness of a shadow is intensified if the sky itself is very blue. You can try this out by painting an object first outside and then indoors, as I have done here.

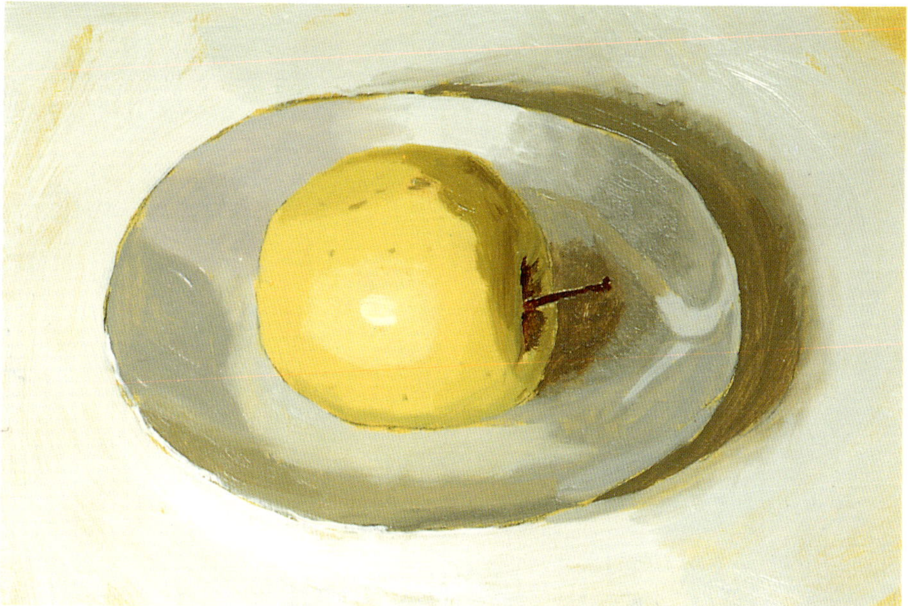

ABOVE

I then painted the same object indoors, illuminated by a white overcast sky through the window. The contours of the shadow are no longer clean-cut since the light source is now diffused. The shadow receives its color from the reflected light in the room.

SKY COLORS

IT IS AN ODD fact that the bluer and flatter you paint the sky, the less convincing it looks. We are so used to describing skies to ourselves in terms of blue or gray that we often fail to notice what kind of blue or gray they are, or how light or dark. I use very complicated mixtures for skies, and I always start by establishing the tone. I do this by holding up a brush with a paint mixture on it, which immediately tells me whether the color I have mixed is too light or too dark. I then continue mixing until it is correct both in tone and color. I find that once I have got the sky right the rest of the painting falls into place, as this acts as a key against which to judge other colors and tones.

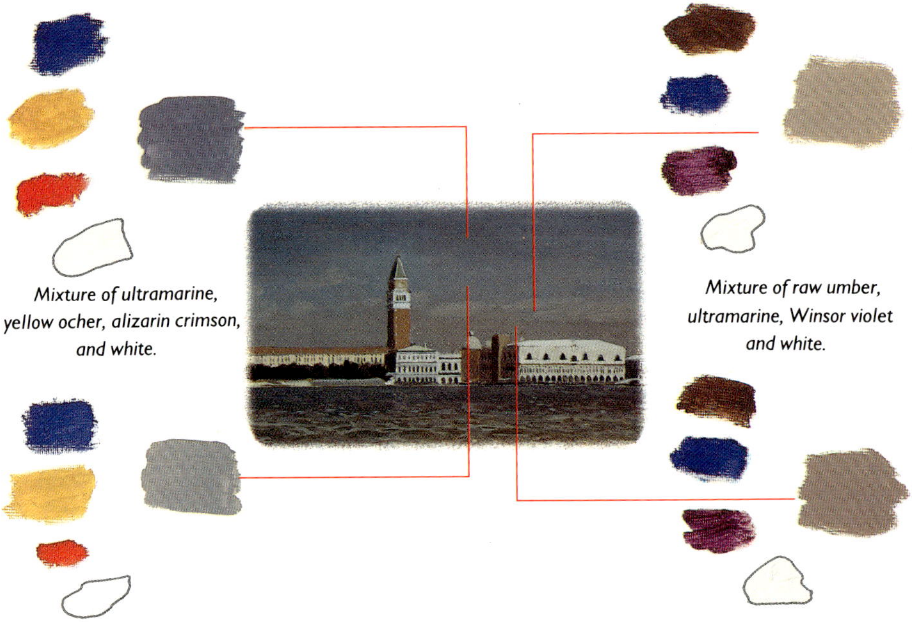

Mixture of ultramarine, yellow ocher, alizarin crimson, and white.

Mixture of raw umber, ultramarine, Winsor violet and white.

Mixture is as above, but in different proportions and with more white.

Mixture is as above, but with more raw umber and white.

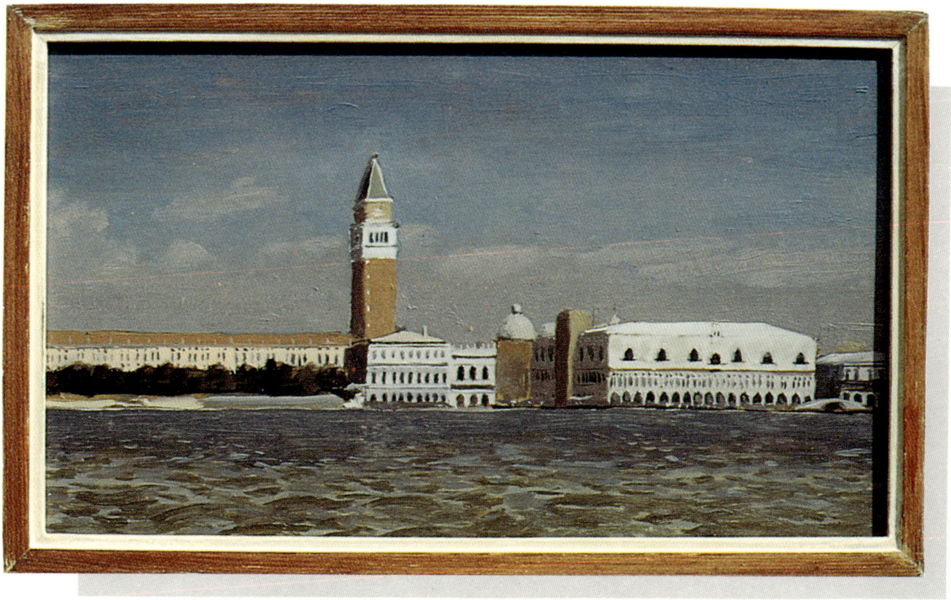

ABOVE AND OPPOSITE

It can be surprisingly difficult to analyze sky colors, particularly when there are several different colors of much the same tone produced by light cloud cover, as in this case. Although this sky gives an impression of blueness, there is very little pure blue. The colors range from purplish gray at the top, to a slightly green-gray at the bottom – there is usually more yellow in clouds above the horizon. The swatches opposite show some of the mixtures used.

SKIN COLORS

FOR SOME REASON people are often afraid of painting skin, but in fact it is no more difficult than anything else. If you tried the white still life exercise on pages 42–3, you may even find skin easier. The trick is first to establish what kind of overall skin color the person has. Half-close your eyes so that you cut out distracting details such as features, and see whether the overall color is pinkish, yellowish, creamy, brownish and so on, and then decide how you would mix a "base color." Once you have this you can often paint the shadows and highlights by varying the proportions of the component colors, perhaps adding touches of blue or green as occasion demands.

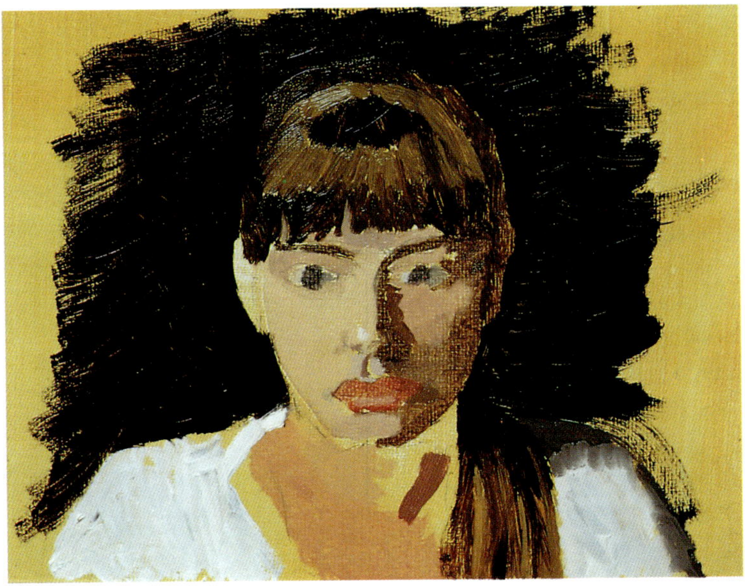

1 My basic mixture, which you can see on the sitter's right cheek and the side of her neck, is raw umber, alizarin crimson, and white. For the shadowed side of the face and neck I have used the same colors, with a higher proportion of raw umber, and additional alizarin in places.

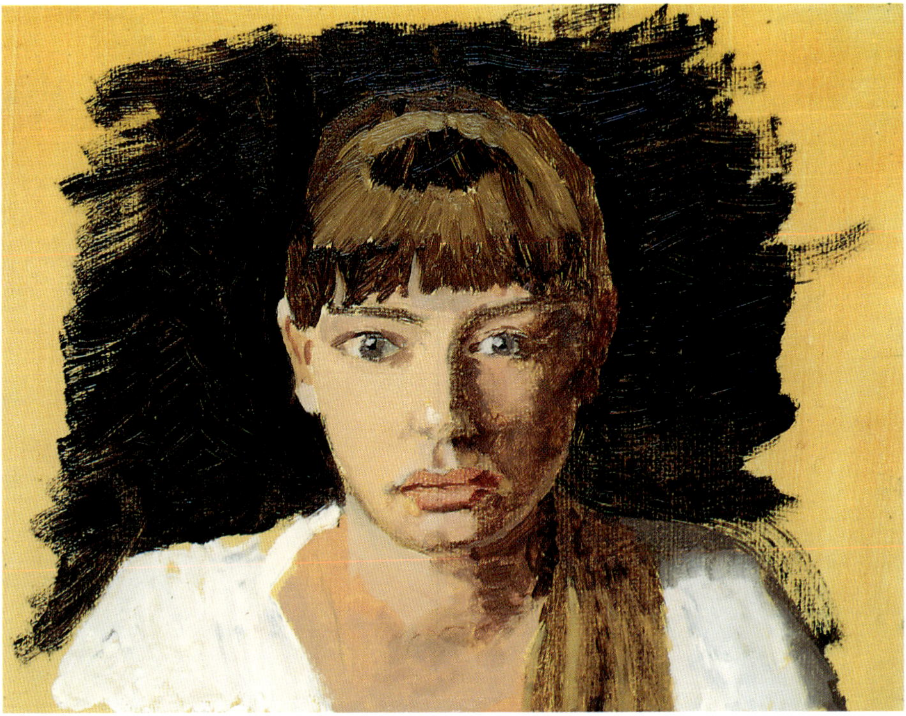

2 In the final stages I added a little yellow ocher to warm the light side of the face and soften the shadows.

GLAZING

GLAZING IS A METHOD often used for painting subjects such as skin and flowers, where you want a transparent, luminous effect. This is a traditional oil-painting technique that was at one time more or less abandoned, but it is now enjoying a revival.

Glazing involves building up colors in a series of transparent layers so that each new color is modified by the one below. Glazing can create lovely effects and offers an alternative way of mixing colors, giving a very different effect from that of opaque colors mixed on

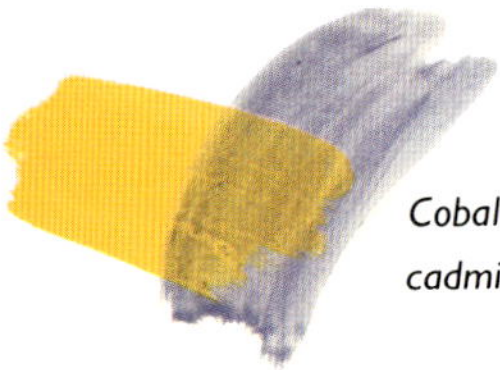

Cobalt blue over cadmium yellow.

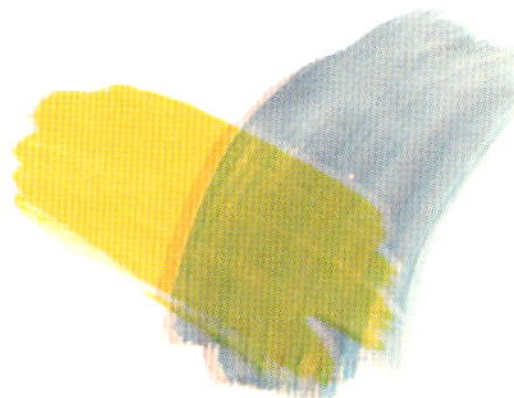

Winsor (phthalocyanine) blue over cadmium yellow.

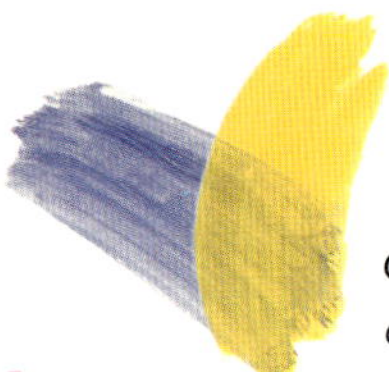

Cadmium yellow over cobalt blue.

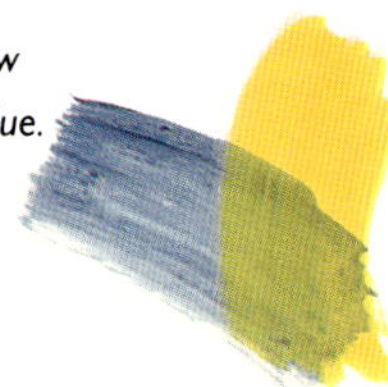

Cadmium yellow over monestial blue.

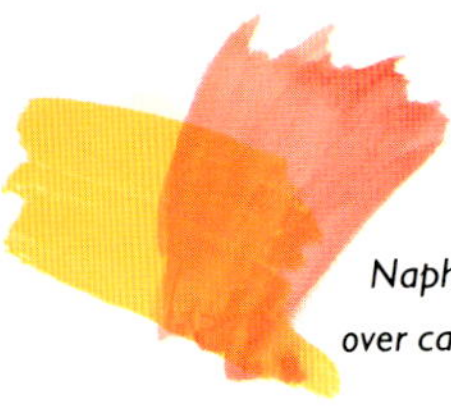

Naphthol crimson over cadmium yellow.

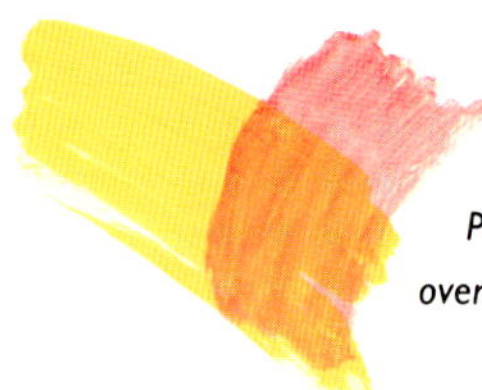

Permanent rose over cadmium yellow.

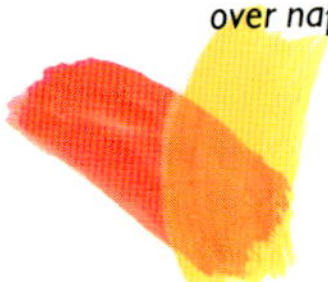

Cadmium yellow over naphthol crimson.

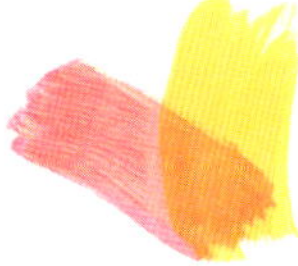

Cadmium yellow over permanent rose.

the palette. Here I have shown some of the possibilities for mixtures, but you can also build up deep, rich individual colors by glazing successive layers of red, for example, or blue. The swatches shown below were executed in acrylic, thinned with water, but you can glaze with oils, too, provided that you use a glazing medium – ask in your art shop if you are not sure what to buy. The only problem is that glazing takes longer with oils, because each layer must be thoroughly dry before the next one is applied.

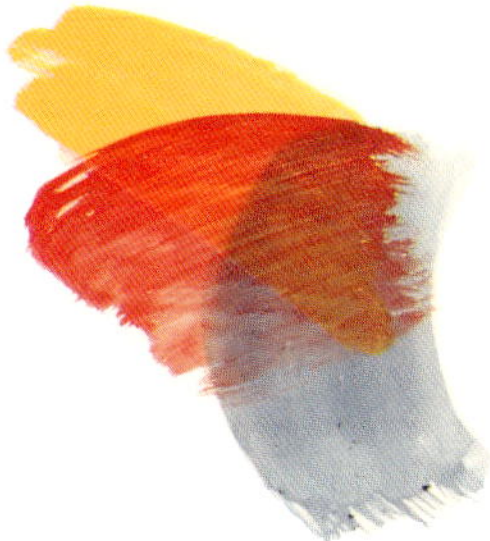

Winsor (phthalocyanine) blue over naphthol crimson over cadmium yellow.

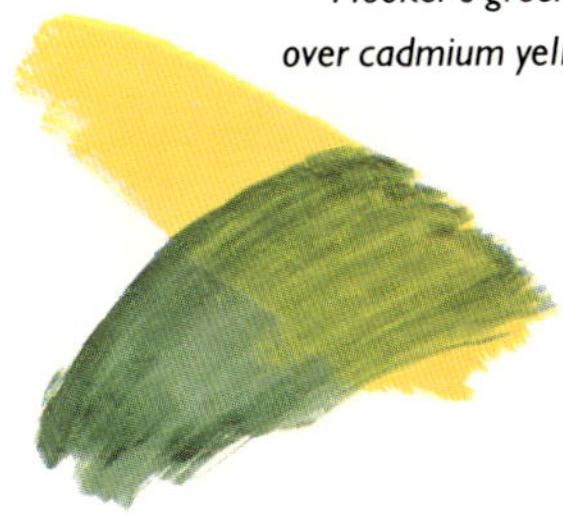

Hooker's green over cadmium yellow.

Cadmium yellow over dioxozine purple.

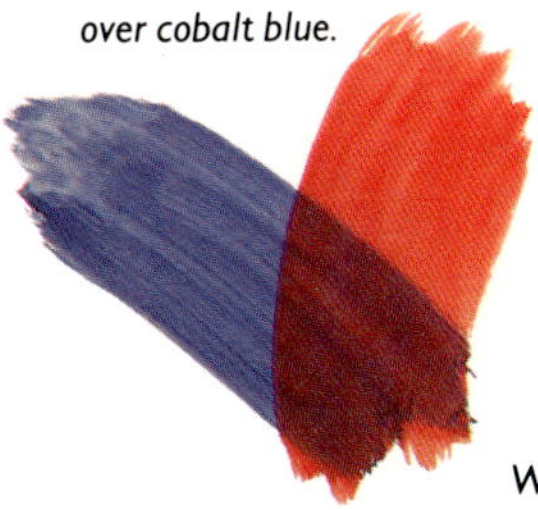

Naphthol crimson over cobalt blue.

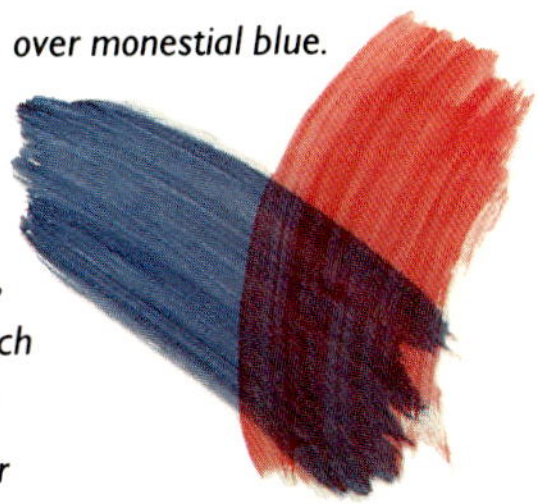

Permanent rose over monestial blue.

ABOVE AND OPPOSITE

When one transparent color is laid over another, mixtures are produced on the picture surface, which can create lovely effects. The same technique is used by watercolor painters, although watercolor glazes are more commonly known as washes.

EXPRESSIVE COLOR

WHEN YOU FIRST start to paint, your main concern will be with representing what you see – learning to analyze and mix colors so that you can give a good account of the visual world. But color can be used in a more personal way: you can heighten or "key up" colors; you can decide to use only light colors or only dark ones; or you can ignore the real colors and invent your own. All these are ways of creating a "mood" in a painting. Light colors generally give a

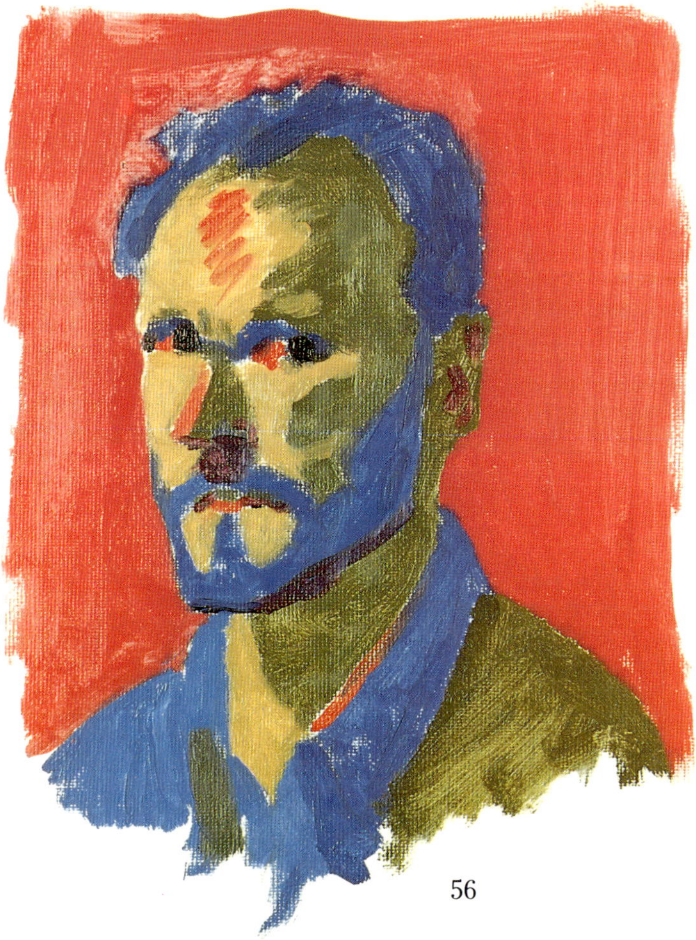

LEFT

Although the colors are not naturalistic, they describe the forms of the face very well because green – a cool, receding color – has been used for the shadowed side of the face, and warm yellows for the light-struck areas. It can be interesting to experiment with "keying up" colors in this way.

happy, cheerful impression. Bright ones can also be cheerful but are more assertive, sometimes even aggressive, depending on the kinds of contrast you use. Dark, heavy colors give a somber feeling, while neutrals are restful – they are unassertive but pleasant to have around. Try a series of self-portraits in different "colorways," as I have done in the pictures below; or ask a friend to pose for you and then use various combinations of color.

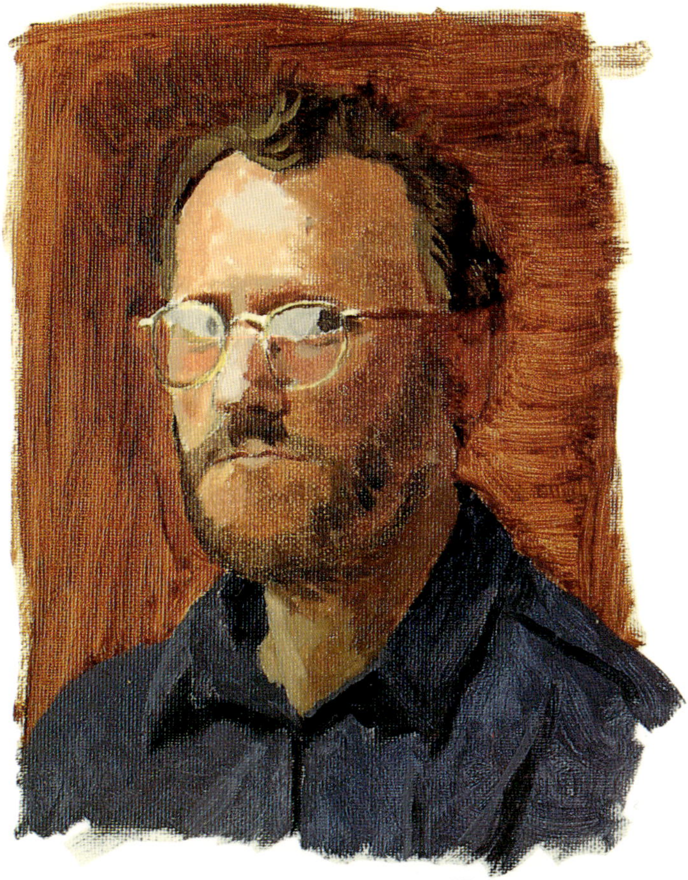

LEFT

Dark tones and muted colors do not always create a depressing effect – because they are unassertive, they can be pleasantly restful. This kind of color scheme is a natural choice for many portraits.

DEMONSTRATION

I AM WORKING in oils, as I nearly always do, on a piece of ordinary mounting board, which I have prepared and tinted with yellow ocher. I like a smooth surface, as I find that the texture of canvas and canvas board interferes with the detail. I do not like to work on a white board since it makes it difficult to judge the first colors you put on – almost any color looks dark by comparison. However, my color-matching system largely prevents me from making any mistakes over color or tone. What I do is to paint bands of

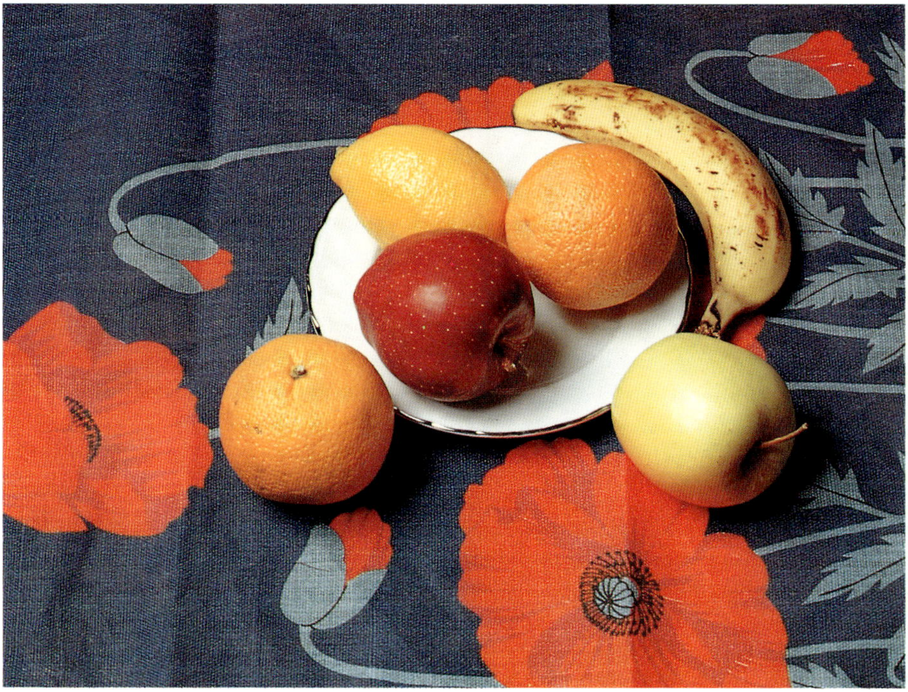

1 The still life set up on a patterned cloth.

color of varying strength on a palette knife and hold it up to the subject, adjusting it so that the light on the knife is the same as that on the subject. As soon as one of the bands coincides with the actual colour I know it is correct. I always begin a painting in this way, making further such checks as I go along. The colors used were ultramarine, sap green, raw sienna, yellow ocher, raw umber, black, cadmium yellow, lemon yellow, alizarin crimson, cadmium red, and titanium white.

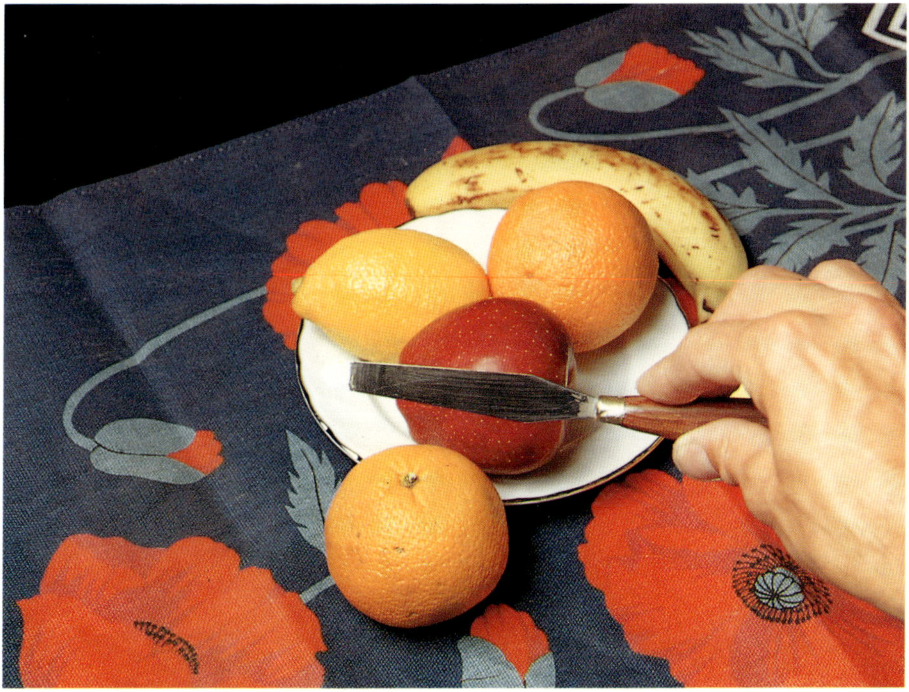

2 I begin with a "key" color, in this case the white of the plate, which is the lightest area of the group. The white on the palette knife has been modified with a little raw umber.

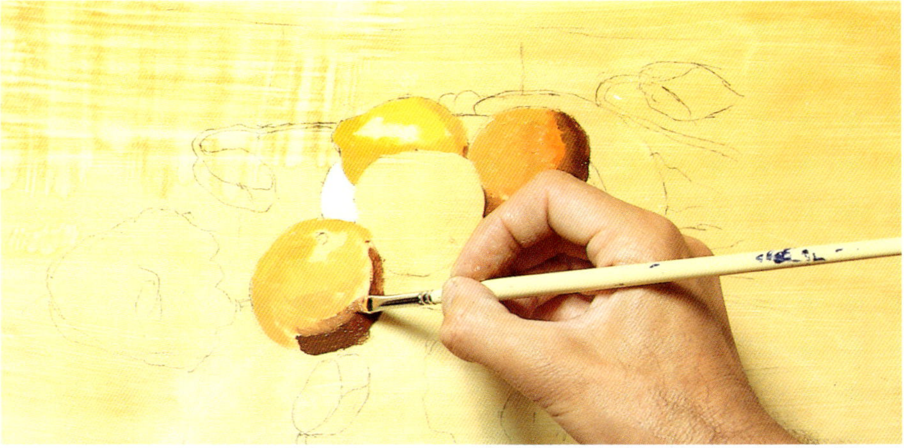

3 Having painted in the white, I now work on the fruit. For the oranges I am using a cadmium red and cadmium yellow mixture in varying proportions, with extra white for the highlights. For the shadows, I have added alizarin crimson, raw umber, and a tiny amount of sap green.

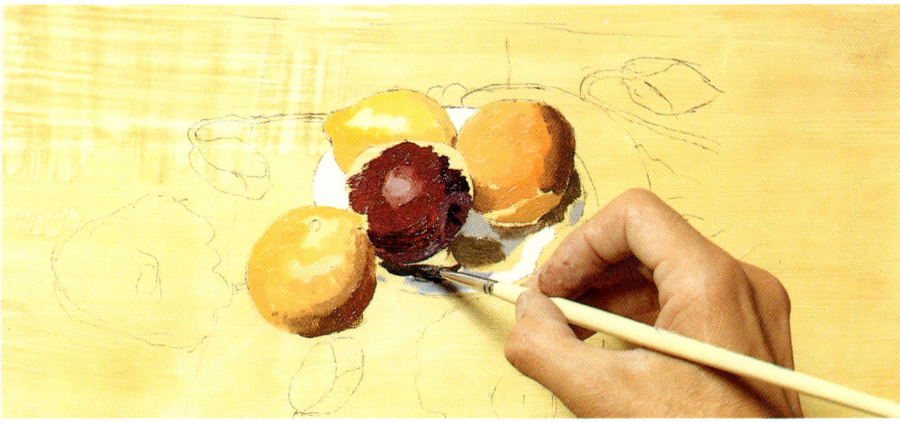

4 The lemon is lemon yellow, cadmium yellow and white, and the apple mainly alizarin crimson, deepened and made slightly blue with ultramarine.

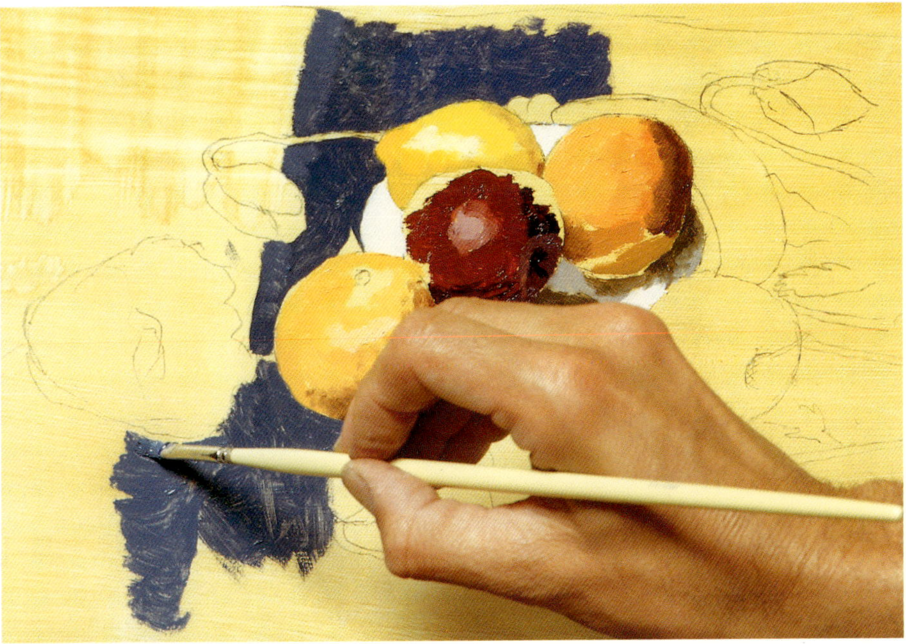

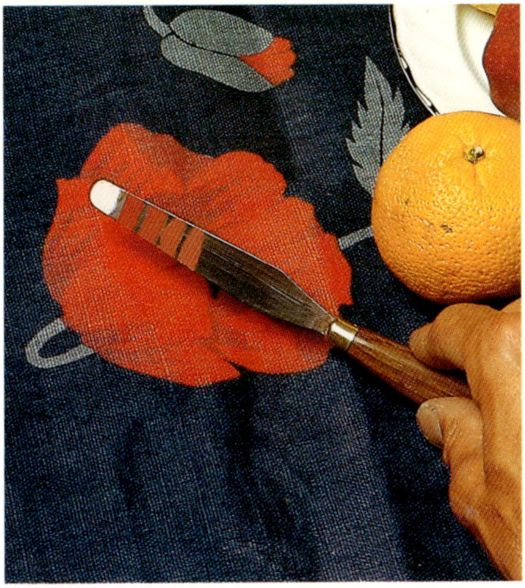

5 With the colors of the fruit now established, I turn my attention to the tablecloth. For this color I have mixed raw umber and white with ultramarine.

6 It is important to capture exactly the brilliant red of the poppies on the tablecloth, since these dominate the painting. I again use my color matching method, painting bands of red on the palette knife and holding it against the actual cloth.

7 I am using cadmium red darkened with alizarin crimson and a small touch of black – too much will neutralize the red and turn it into brown.

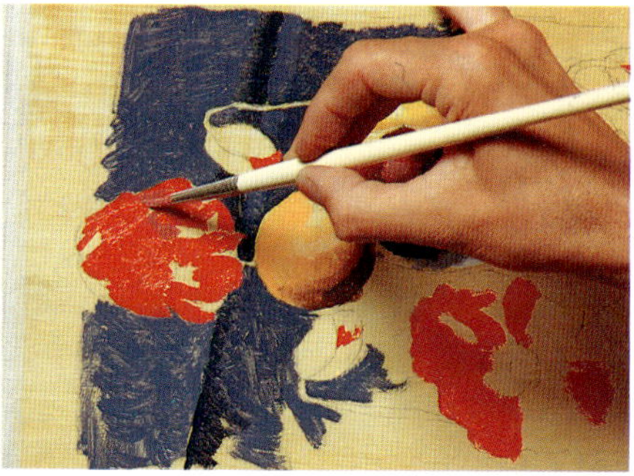

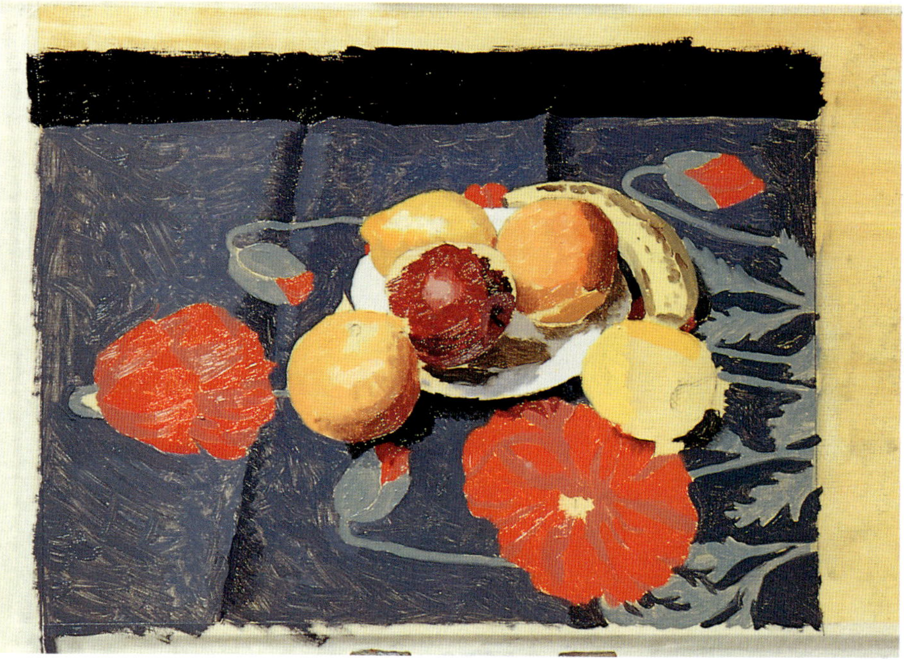

8 Notice that I have not taken the painting to the edges of the board. The advantage of working on thin board rather than canvas is that you can change the format. When I want to frame the picture, I simply trim off the edges.

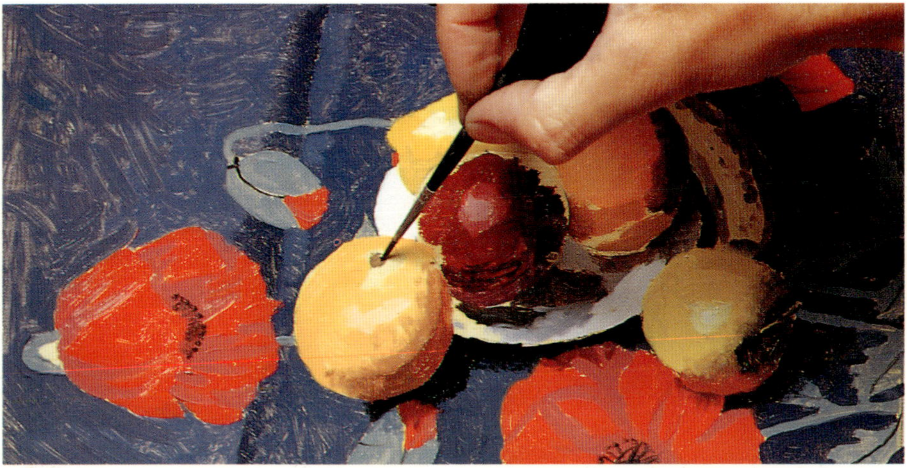

9 The painting is nearly finished; all it needs is a few small details, such as the pit at the top of the orange. The placing of this is important since it helps to define the shape of the fruit.

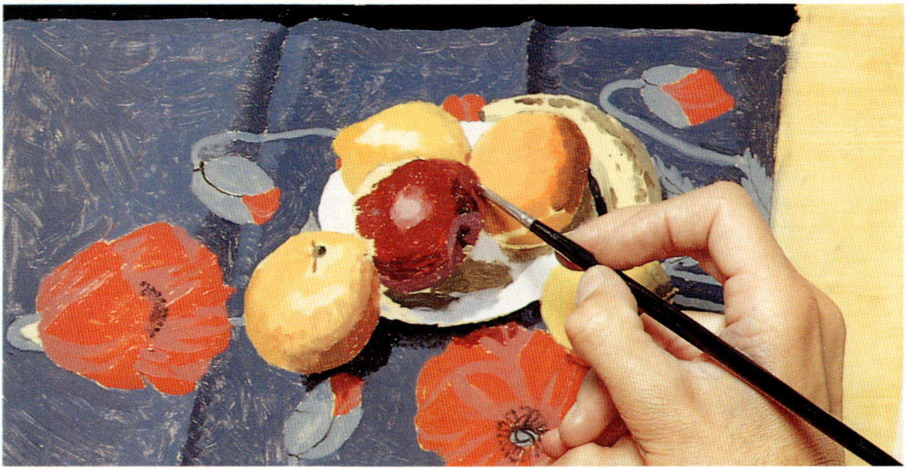

10 Finally, I complete the apple, using a little yellow ocher in my crimson mixture for the reflected light bouncing back from the orange.

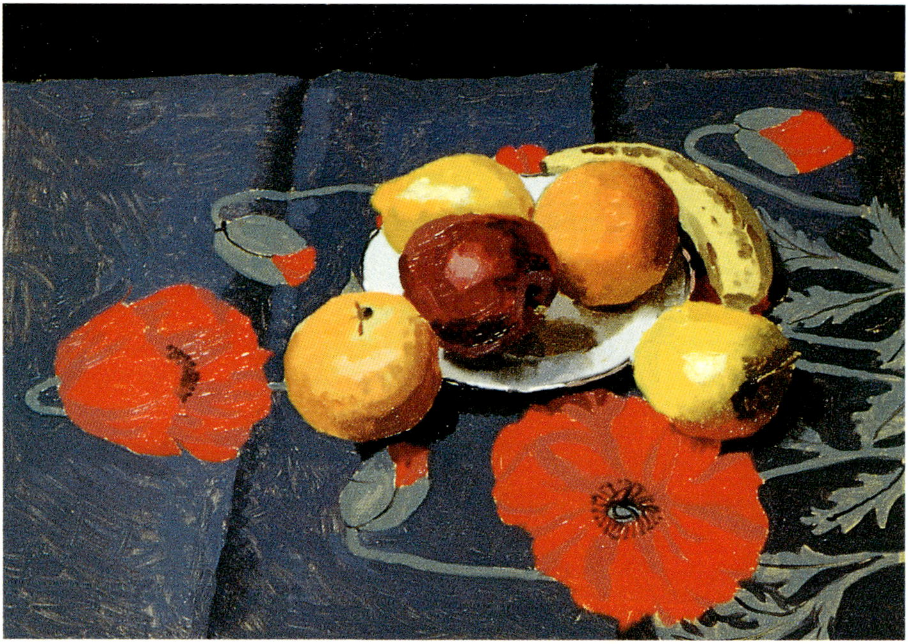

11 After some final tidying up, the painting is now complete.

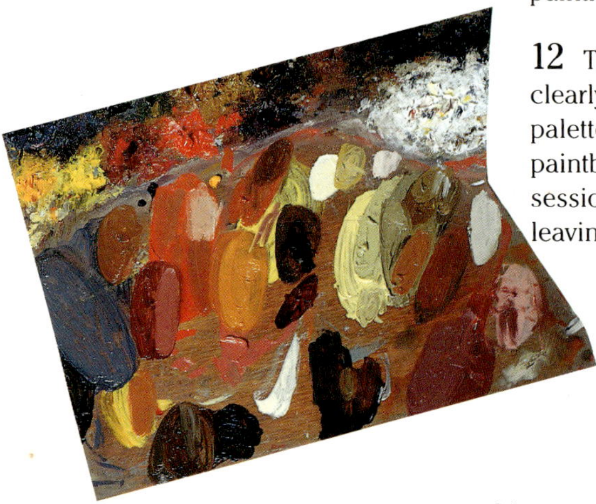

12 The palette shows the mixtures clearly. I use a rectangular wooden palette that fits into the lid of my paintbox. At the end of a working session I clean only the mixing area, leaving the colors in place at the top.